101 Smart
QUESTIONS
TO ASK
ON YOUR
INTERVIEW

BY RON FRY

THOMSON

DELMAR LEARNING

THOMSON

DELMAR LEARNING

101 Smart Questions to Ask on Your Interview
by Ron Fry

COPYRIGHT © 2003 by Ron Fry
Printed in Canada
2 3 4 5 XXX 05 04

For more information contact
Delmar Learning
Executive Woods 5 Maxwell Drive
Clifton Park,NY 12065-2919

Or you can visit our Internet site at
http://www.delmarlearning.com

Library of Congress Cataloging-in-
Publication
ISBN 1-56414-669-3

NOTICE TO THE READER

CONTENTS

Welcome TO the JUNGLE

"Today's economy requires job hunters to be more proactive, more sophisticated, and more willing to go through brick walls to get what they want. Employers no longer plan your career for you. You must look after yourself, and know what you want and how to get it.

—Kate Wendleton,
Interviewing and Salary Negotiation

Many so-called pundits will reassure you that the job market is never as bad as it seems, even now. There are always companies hiring when others are firing, they proclaim. So even when massive layoffs are announced, there are still opportunities, especially for entry-level or lower-level people who have a unique qualification: They'll work cheaper, just because they're younger and/or less skilled.

Well, as I sit finalizing this introduction (in March of 2003), I've got to tell you that this just isn't true. In fact, I don't think it's been true for two to three years. According to outplacement firm Challenger, Gray & Christmas, there have been nearly 3 1/2 million layoffs since March, 2001. And when big companies cut these days, they aren't lopping off 25,000 employees with one hand and welcoming 10,000 new hires with the other. They're just cutting 25,000 jobs and making everyone who remains work longer and harder.

When will this bloodbath end? I don't think the end is in sight.

First, the bad news...

The days of filling out a two-page employment application, casually chatting your way through one or two friendly interviews, then leisurely sorting through a handful of lucrative offers are long gone. In these tough economic times, interviewers and hiring managers are reluctant to leave anything to chance. Many have begun to experiment with the latest techniques for data-gathering and analysis. For many employers, especially the biggest, interviewing has become a full-fledged science.

This means interviewing is a real challenge for you: You are faced with the task of convincing a total stranger to invest company money and time in you, when, more than likely, his budget has been slashed...and slashed...and slashed again. The pressure on interviewers to ensure that only the best possible candidates are hired is overwhelming.

Believe me, you won't be reading any stories about Stanford MBAs starting new companies in their dorm rooms and mulling over multi-million dollar venture capital deals. The remnants of the dotcom bust are still smoldering, Wall Street is hoping its averages don't head south for the fifth year in a row, consumer confidence is still stuck somewhere between slim and none, most of us are still recovering from 9/11, and no one expects the hiring environment to improve in the near term.

Now the worse news...

Yes, selling yourself into the highly competitive market that currently exists is a difficult prospect. But that's not all. You're more likely to contend with a tougher interview than even a couple of years ago because of the rapidly increasing sophistication of those doing the hiring. Corporations are spending more money than ever on psychological tests, honesty tests, drug tests, assessments, and computerized screening systems.

They are sending recruiters and supervisors to courses on interviewing and candidate-evaluation procedures. They are using new interviewing techniques, some of which would make thumbscrews seem like an attractive alternative. And they are subjecting *you* to more and longer interviews.

Although it would be unrealistic to expect any new hire, no matter how experienced, to be accompanied by an ironclad guarantee, many employers are taking the extra steps they deem necessary to ensure they do not even *consider* hiring someone who won't start contributing to the bottom line from day one. They can afford to be choosy, and they've found better ways to choose. They are seeking self-managing employees who are versatile, confident, not afraid to roll up their sleeves and get the job done...and they're going to probably try to pay them less. And *don't* ask about bonuses.

A little ray of hope

Despite this doom and gloom scenario, for the prepared candidate, the interview process is still a two-way street. There *are* still tremendous opportunities available for candidates who are ready to ace the interview process.

Like *you*.

Most job candidates think of the interview in completely the wrong way. They think of it as an interrogation, a police line-up. And they see themselves as suspects, not as the key prospects they really are.

This book will show you that you are, to a very large degree, *in charge of the interview*. It will convince you that you are there not only to sell the company on *you*, but to make sure that *you* are sold on *them*. It will give you the powerful questions that will work whatever your age, whatever your experience, whatever your goals.

It will *not*, however, spend very much time preparing you for the questions the interviewer is going to throw at *you*. Luckily for you (why am I so good to you?), I've already written the companion book to this one—*101 Great Answers to the Toughest Interview Questions*—whose sole purpose is to do exactly that. (Not only did I already write it, I've already revised it three times, and it's already sold a million copies.) Using these books together, you will be amply armed for any interview and any interviewer.

Even though I think you should buy a copy of that other title, I am going to reveal a secret that may cost me sales: There really aren't 101 questions you have to prepare yourself for. Not even a dozen. There are only four (with a couple of variations thrown in):

Can you do the job? (Are you specifically qualified?)

Will **you do the job** (better than the other people I'm interviewing)?

Will you actually *take* the job if I offer it to you? How hungry are you? How much do you actually want *this* specific job?

Even if you are perfectly qualified and highly motivated, do I think you will fit in with the rest of the group?

The smaller the company or department, the more important this "chemistry" question becomes.

Will you make me, the interviewer, look like a genius for recommending or hiring you?

Or will your screw-ups and missteps make me look like an idiot, kill my promotion, slash my bonus, maybe even jeopardize my own job? (The higher up on the food chain the interviewer is, the more central this question becomes to her.)

Why ask questions?

Crafting concise, targeted, enthusiastic, and positive responses to the interviewer's questions gives you an opportunity to demonstrate your knowledge of the company and industry and to show how your qualifications would make you fit right in. *Asking* concise, targeted, and well-crafted questions gives you more chances to demonstrate the extent of your research, to build on whatever rapport you've established, and to align what you can offer with what the company needs.

And, by their very nature, they proclaim that *you are interested*. Likewise, the complete *lack* of questions will unanimously convince interviewers that you are *not* interested.

Oh, you *were* interested? You just didn't *have* any questions. Sorry, interviewers don't consider that an option. No questions? No job offer. That's certainly a rule with a vast majority of interviewers. (No, no, please, don't try the "but the interviewer was so good, he answered all my questions" bit. Doesn't work. Wouldn't be prudent. Not going to go there.)

As I'm going to emphasize throughout this book, asking questions the smart way is just another way to match your skills, talents, and qualifications to the company's needs, another opportunity to demonstrate that you are far and away the only candidate the interviewer should consider. By preceding many of your questions with a phrase or statement that reminds the interviewer of something you said earlier or a point you want to continually reemphasize, it is another opportunity to "blow your own horn":

> *"Mr. Jones, as my stint at Eubonics, Inc. clearly shows, I have the ability to motivate a team to overachieve, but could you tell me a little more about the individuals I'd be working with here?"*

How to construct smart questions

Let me save the obsessive-compulsives among you some time—there are far more than 101 smart questions in this book. How do I know (because *I* didn't count them!)? While there may be 101 general questions in the book (although I *think* there are quite a few more), there are a near-infinite number of specific, qualifying, clarifying questions you can ask. I intend to point you in the right direction, but the details of such questions are going to be determined by your exact situation, by what you've said during the interview and by what the interviewer has said. How much (or little) research you've done will also expand (or limit) the depth and breadth of your questions.

Here's an example of how to construct dozens of great questions after asking a general question and receiving a relatively innocuous reply from the interviewer:

You: *"Mr. Barton, I noticed in the latest issue of Publisher's Weekly that you intend to increase the number of books you publish next year from 50 to 72."*

Him: *"Yes, we do."* (Lot of detail there. Really something to grab onto. Did it hurt him to talk so long and give you so much information?)

Here are just *some* of the questions that would naturally evolve from this initial exchange:

> *"Why did you make that decision?"*
> *"Who made that decision?"*

"Do you know what categories the additional books will be published in?"

"How did you settle on 22 additional books?"

"Are you going to publish in categories other than your traditional ones?"

"Do you have a feel for the kinds of new books you're seeking?"

"How would that expansion affect my position? My department? My superior? My subordinates?"

"Is my position being created, in whole or in part, because of that decision?"

"Will others have to be hired as well? In what departments?"

"Does this mean the company believes the economy is ready to grow again?"

"What is the mix of the new books, in terms of fiction and nonfiction?"

"Is the company able to fund this expansion without going to the capital markets—I know last year was not a particularly good one for many publishers."

I could go on and on. And, in fact, for every answer Mr. Barton gives to each of the previous questions, another half dozen questions would easily spring to mind. Follow-up questions are the heart and soul of the interview process...*from both sides of the desk.*

While I'll be talking much more about how to phrase follow-up questions in the chapters to come, let me point out one thing our hypothetical candidate did in a couple of the previous questions: *She assumed the position.* In other words, she referred to *"my* department," *"my* superiors," and *"my* position," *implying that the job was already hers.* Such a subtle strategy may have no effect if she is otherwise unqualified for the job, but it *may* turn out to be the "tipping point" if she winds up neck-and-neck with another candidate.

So, do you have any questions?

Normally, this question occurs very near the end of the interview. In fact, you may well assume that its appearance pretty much signals the end.

But do you have to wait until the interviewer puts you through the wringer, smiles benevolently, and actually asks, "So, do you have any questions?" I really don't think so, but there are a couple of caveats to keep in mind before you charge ahead with your best Barbara Walters impression:

Always ask permission to ask the first couple of questions. Once it's clear the interviewer has no problem with *your* asking questions, even as she continues to pepper you with her own, you will have established a flow and won't need to ask permission each time. But it's up to you to make sure the interviewer is comfortable with your approach. If he shows obvious signs of discomfort— frowning while muttering "Okay," pursing his lips, or showing in any other way that he is *not* too keen on your interrupting his supposedly well-crafted approach to the interview session—back off!

But if an interviewer suggests you are free to ask questions at any time or tells you it's fine when you ask permission, do so! In that case, waiting for the ubiquitous *"Do you have any questions?"* is a bad move: The interviewer may have already downgraded you because you *didn't* take her (strong) hint to be assertive right from the start.

Asking questions during the regular interview **does not** mean interrupting. And it doesn't mean always answering an interviewer's question with a question of your own, which may well thwart the interviewer's attempts to assess your strengths. (And you don't want to thwart him, do you?).

Taking the initiative and asking questions early (with the interviewer's permission, of course) is the scenario I prefer, both as an interviewee and an interviewer.

As an interviewer, it impresses me. It makes me believe (barring evidence to the contrary) that the person in front of me is interested, engaged, and assertive.

As an interviewee, I want to control the interview, and asking questions early and often certainly accomplishes that. Doing so is especially effective with an inept (or at least less-than-veteran) interviewer, who may welcome your help!

Another great reason to ask questions early and often is because it transforms a stilted, traditional "Q&A"—with you being the "A"—into a *conversation*. By definition, this makes the meeting less formal, less "you vs. me," more "we." A conversation is how you explore areas of common interest, trade comments, chat rather than "talk." In other words, the way you establish the chemistry that is one of the vital factors in landing any job!

Last but not least, asking a good question is a slick way to sidestep an uncomfortable question from the interviewer (at least for the time being). Why did you have that one year gap in your resume? Darn. You didn't want to have to talk about that aborted dotcom bomb *yet*. Don't expect the topic to die. You are probably just buying a temporary respite. But at least you've given yourself a little time to think how you want to handle it.

How to use this book

It's as important to know how and when to ask a question as it is to know which questions to ask. In Chapter 1, we'll talk about questioning "strategy"—general rules to follow to ensure your questions are concise, appropriate, timely and to-the-point. Oh, and that they actually accomplish what you want them to.

Chapter 2 is, in my mind, the most important in the book even though it has nothing to do with questions to ask on your interview. More importantly, it details questions to ask *yourself* before you even make a phone call, answer an ac', meet with a recruiter, or send out a resume. It won't do you much good to have a list of fantastic questions to ask an interviewer if you're seeking the wrong job at the wrong company in the wrong industry! Chapter 2 will ensure you take the time to analyze who you are, what's important to you, and what you ideally want in a job and a career.

Once you know where you're going, Chapter 3 will give you the help you need to begin researching the companies you intend to target.

In Chapter 4, you'll start constructing the smart questions to ask "pre-interviewers"—employment agencies, recruiters, headhunters and Human Resources—who can't say yes, but can certainly say no!

Finally in Chapters 5, 6, and 7, you'll be ready to concentrate on the questions to ask the hiring manager—the person who can actually say those magic words, "You're hired! When can you start?"

Chapter 5 covers basic questions about the company, department, and job; probing questions designed to elicit more and more detail; style questions about your potential boss and the corporate culture; and pre-closing questions to get a better feel for how the interview is going and what you need to do to land the job.

In Chapter 6, I give you a series of great closing questions—to identify hidden objections, find out about the other candidates (your competition), and push for an offer.

Finally, in Chapter 7, I'll tell you what to do when you actually receive a job offer, how to get the best deal—when and how to discuss salary, bonuses, benefits and perks— and how to maximize your compensation package. I'll also discuss how to handle the rejections endemic to the job-search process.

Enough preparation. Let's get busy.

Chapter 1

When, Where, Why, AND How TO ASK Smart QUESTIONS

I'm going to assume that you have already been on enough interviews (or, if you're a recent graduate, read enough interviewing books) to know that there are rules to follow during interviews. So, I'm not going to discuss them here.

However, there is a list of "no-no's" that are so important that failing to avoid them can virtually doom *any* chance you have of securing the job before the interview even starts. Given their seriousness, I thought it prudent to remind you of them:

- ❑ Poor grooming.

- ❑ Inappropriate dress.

- ❑ Showing up late (or not showing up at all!)

- ❑ An answer, good and specific or not, that simply does not answer the question asked.

- ❑ Defensiveness, especially if it's about something that doesn't appear to *need* defending.

❏ Lack of knowledge of the company, job, and/or industry (or any other evidence of poor or nonexistent preparation and research).

❏ Dishonesty.

❏ Lack of enthusiasm/interest.

❏ Asking the wrong questions (at the wrong time of the wrong people).

❏ Any answer that reveals you are clearly unqualified for the job.

❏ Any question that reveals you have little or no understanding of the job.

❏ Any disparity between your resume/cover letter and interview answers (such as providing details about jobs not on your resume).

❏ Lack of focus.

❏ Lack of eye contact.

❏ Any negativity, especially in discussing people (your last boss, co-workers).

❏ Any question or answer that makes it obvious you do not intend to take responsibility for failures/weaknesses/bad decisions/bad results.

❏ Any question or answer that makes it clear you intend to take full credit for a project/result/success to which others undoubtedly contributed.

Many interviewers may not consider any one of these an automatic reason for dismissal; an accumulation of two or more may force even the most empathetic to question your suitability. (Some items, of course, such as dishonesty, may well lead to an immediate and heartfelt "Thank you...please *don't* stay in touch.")

The art of questioning

Before we start delving into specific questions to ask yourself, "pre-interviewers," and the hiring manager, let's agree on some overarching rules, if you will, that will govern them.

Shape your questions to the position.

Learn as much as you can about the position for which you're interviewing—*before* you show up for *any* interview. When you ask questions about any aspect of the industry, company, department, or job, make sure they are couched in terms of the requirements of the specific job you're seeking, and the goals of the particular company at which you hope to be hired.

Don't ask about time off.

At least not before you're offered the job.

Don't ask about salary or benefits.

Again, wait until you are offered the job. (See Chapter 7 to understand why.) You don't want money to be a factor when the interviewer is still wondering whether you're the best person for the job...even worthy of a callback.

Know what to ask when of whom

Questions differ depending on both where you are in the interviewing process—screening interview, hiring interview, first, second, third, etc.—and, during a particular interview, where you are in the interviewer's script.

The earlier you are in the process, the more likely you'll be asking general questions about where the company's going, its culture, what it deems important or valuable. Your questions are an attempt to get an initial feel for how you'd fit in, where you'd fit in, whether and how you could grow, etc.

The more time you devote to a particular company, the more targeted and probing the questions should become, both the interviewer's of you and those you ask the interviewer. You'll really want to start honing in on the particular information you need to decide whether this is the right company, position and boss for you. So the farther along in the process, the more individualized the questions become (because what's most important to you may be something I wouldn't even ask about, such as the availability of on-site daycare, reimbursement of moving expenses or tuition, etc.).

Get the interviewer talking

Ask open-ended questions—those that begin with "Who," "What," "When," "Where," or "How." Your purpose is to establish a conversation, to get the interviewer talking so he volunteers the information you want (and just maybe, to elicit some information you don't even *know* you want). These kinds of questions do that. Closed-ended questions—those that can be answered by a simple "yes" or "no," and undoubtedly will be—are useful near the end of an interview, when you want to "close" the sale, or when you *do* want specific answers to specific questions. "Do I have to wait 90 days for medical coverage?" A simple "yes" or "no" will do fine.

"Why" questions can be a little tricky, because if you're not sensitive, they can make you come off as more aggressive than you might possibly want: "I noticed you put a lot of books out of print last year. Why did you do that?"

You can extract the same information in a gentler way: "It seems from your annual report that more books than usual were remaindered last year. Was that mainly the effect of 9/11?"

Ask probing questions, usually open-ended, to extract more details and to follow up after general questions.

Consider asking questions that aren't questions. This is a way to put a nervous interviewer at ease by making a statement rather than asking pointed queries. It takes some practice, but it's very effective in getting reluctant interviewers to open up: "What would help me most would be to get a better feel for the culture I'd be walking into and the styles of the people with whom I'd be working. Could you take a couple of minutes to give me a better understanding of those issues?"

Match your style to the interviewer's

That doesn't mean you have to become a total milquetoast when interviewing with a fairly passive interviewer, but, if facing such a scenario, it may behoove you to tone down the "sales killer" personality a bit.

That's why you have to be a little careful about a "one-size-fits-all" interview approach. Yes, employers want go-getters, confident candidates, enthusiastic hard workers. But take the time to look around whatever office you're visiting. Is everyone pretty laid back? Then don't come on like a house afire! You can still crow about the results you achieved without scaring everyone!

Likewise, if you're inherently reluctant to blow your own horn anyway and are a little passive and laid back yourself, an atmosphere akin to a penny stock boiler room might not be your cup of tea, even if they *are* looking for a "detail-oriented accountant type."

Watch the interviewer's body language

You also need to always gauge the interviewer's response to what you're saying, not just the answers you've given but the questions you've asked. Listen for verbal clues and watch the body language that will often tell you how you're *really* doing. If it's obvious you've hit a wrong note, you may even want to say something like: "I'm sorry. That question seemed to make you uncomfortable. Is that an area you're not yet prepared to talk about?" Again, you don't want to kill a potential job because you were overly aggressive on the interview.

If you know what to look for, you'll get extra clues from the body language of an interviewer:

❏ **Lack of eye contact or "shifting" eyes** are usually seen as a sign of dishonesty or, at best, discomfort: *"Mr. Interviewer, are you planning any more layoffs?"* Squint, shift, shift, shift. *"Uh, no, Jim. So, how about those Bucs?"*

❏ **Raised eyebrows** indicate disbelief or even mild distain, along the lines of *"Oh, really?" "You don't mean that, do you?" "Gee, how'd you figure that out?"* or *"You don't actually expect me to buy that, do you?"*

❏ **A smile at the wrong time** can be a sign of discomfort or an indication of a complete lack of appropriate social skills!

❏ **"Closed" positions of the hands and arms**—clenched fists, arms folded across the body—are not positive. They may also indicate boredom.

❏ An interviewer who is **slumping or leaning** back in his chair may be showing disrespect (arrogance) or disinterest. It is surely a sign that you have to ask a question to get him back into the conversation and his "head" back to your candidacy.

❏ Doodling, chewing on a pencil, scratching, playing with one's hands, moving things around on a desk, or acting distracted are typical **signs of nervousness.** Don't interpret these as anything more than nerves unless something else tips you off. Again, ask a question to get the focus back on you or, even better, a question about *them.* Everyone likes to talk about themselves, especially a not-too-experienced interviewer who seems to be nervous about interviewing *you,* believe it or not!

Be concise and to-the-point

If your question is so long that even *you* don't remember the beginning by the time you finally reach the end, what do you expect the poor interviewer to do? Ask one question at a time, not a series of questions masquerading as a multi-clause construction. Then, follow up with a series of equally pointed and specific questions to elicit more information.

Assume the position

Even when my brother, Ken, was a relatively low-level salesperson at his current company, he constantly talked about what "we" were doing and how "we" were doing it and what "our" prospects were. Despite the fact that he was not privy to the executive ranks, what "they" knew or where "they" were headed, his use of "we" certainly gave the impression he was more involved in those decisions than he was...and he wasn't involved at all in any of them!

It must have worked. He's now the president of the company.

Learn from my bro. When appropriate, assume you already have the job and ask questions accordingly:

> *"Mr. Baines, what's the first challenge **we're** going to face together?*
>
> *"Ms. Lyndon, what projections do **we** need to hit next year?"*
>
> *"Mr. Johnson, what are the three most important targets you have for **my** department?"*

Don't ask questions that show your ignorance

...or your lack of good research, poor sense of taste, or strange sense of humor. And don't ask questions that are just plain wacko:

> *"Mr. Ames, do you really make money selling Nerf balls? Who the heck came up with that nutty notion?"*

> *"Who named the company?"*

> *"Do you think Puerto Rico should become the 51st state?"*

> *"Should I tweeze my eyebrows?"*

Don't ask questions that reveal your biases

> *"Hmm, Blaustein, that's a Jewish name, isn't it?"*

> *"Will I be working with a lot of foreigners? I don't like people babbling in another language."*

> *"Will my boss have a problem taking my suggestions? After all, I did graduate first in my class at MIT, and I understand he barely made it through Jimmy Dean's School of Air Conditioning and Sausage-making."*

Don't make an interviewer obviously uncomfortable

...by asking questions such as the previous biased, ignorant, or just plain weird ones, or those that are too personal (*"Tell me about your children." "Are you married?"*); too desperate (*"I really need to pay the rent by next Friday. If you offer me this job, could I get a loan before I start?")*; or too incredibly arrogant (*"I have a few problems with the offer. May I talk to someone with the authority to give me what I want?"*)

And avoid any question that has nothing whatsoever to do with the job, department, or company. These may include, but are not limited to, asking for a date, inquiring about the "smoking break" policy, or asking any question that would lead even the most understanding interviewer to immediately call security and have you forcefully ejected, preferably from the state.

Don't introduce negativity into an interviewer's mind

There is nothing inherently wrong with asking about normal work hours, as long as you don't say, "My last boss expected me to work most Saturdays. You don't, do you?" Oh, yeah. You are *so* committed.

As I've noted, some questions are perfectly fine but not if asked at the wrong time. When you have been offered a job, it is expected that you will want to know every detail of compensation, vacation schedules, holidays, and all that other practical stuff. But asking about vacation days in the first five minutes of an interview is not recommended.

Don't tell a joke...

...even if you think you're the next Robin Williams.

Most of us think we're a lot funnier than we actually are, and humor is, to murder a metaphor, in the ear of the beholder. Why take a chance that some lame jokes might cost you a job? Be at ease, feel free to smile, and even offer a humorous (or at least less than serious) comment if it seems in keeping with the rest of the conversation. But please remember that you are there to convince them to hire you and assess whether you want to be hired, not to audition for a gig at the Laff Factory.

Never let them see you sweat

Don't ask questions that make you appear desperate...even if you've been terminated from your previous job!

I noticed something truly bizarre during my dating days. When I was young and single and HUNGRY, I seemed to give off vibes that screamed, "Warning! Warning! Women beware. Desperate bachelor on the prowl." Not long after I married, I was out with friends and seemed to suddenly be a rock star. Virtually every single woman in the bar was smiling at me, sending over a drink, making it known that I was their guy.

What the heck was happening? I was never a lady killer, and my okay looks hadn't suddenly changed. George Clooney didn't need to worry about me being in the same room and scarfing up all the available women. Well, my total unscientific, amateur, unsupported premise is that the same "vibes" that had cried desperation were now sending out soothing, happy, content signals...and people were responding the way you would expect them to.

Interviewers, whether men or women, will react in the same way. Be desperate, think desperate, and you might as well walk in carrying a sign saying, "Will work for anyone, do anything, require nothing." That is not the message employers want to hear and, I suspect, not the one you want to be sending them.

This is also a factor when you are trying to find a job, *any* job, and are clearly overqualified for the ones you're pursuing. It's hard to feign interest in a job you don't really care about. Did you pick a "safety" school when you were a high school senior, one you figured you'd have no problem getting into if the places you *really* wanted to go turned you down? Did any of you get *rejected* by your safety schools? Maybe when you interviewed there, you unconsciously sent them the message that they *were* your "safety" school! No employer wants someone who "just wants a job, any job."

Remember it's a two-way street

It's impossible to lead you by the hand through a whole series of potential questions—smart or not—for the simple reason that the specific questions you choose to ask should be an attempt to redefine the job so it more closely fits your qualifications. *HUH?* Let me explain.

In very large companies, job titles and descriptions seem to be etched in stone. But the smaller the company, the more likely there are a plethora of possible duties, not all of which a single person can do. Or not all of which any single person is qualified to do. So, especially at the smaller company (but even at many of the larger ones), you want to attempt to customize the job the employer *thinks* he is offering you so it more closely matches the qualifications you have.

Let me give you an example of how this can work. Career Press has seven editors. One is exclusively acquisitions, meaning he finds the books that the company is going to publish each season (or, at least, develops a solid list from which to choose). The other six are involved in production, everything from working with authors on their manuscripts in a general way—move this chapter, kill that example, add a checklist—to detailed line editing, proofreading, designing the interior "look," then executing that format and getting the book off to the printer.

Not long ago, we needed to hire a new editor. My Editor-in-chief wanted a typical editor—another "word" person who could do initial editing on every manuscript that came in, then pass them off to an editor who would work with each author on the more detailed, line-by-line edits.

But then Jinny walked in and declared, "Look, I can't really edit in a general way. In fact, I'm not really that kind of editor at all. But I *am* the best darned formatter you ever saw. Instead of hiring a general editor, why don't you let the rest of the editors spend more time editing and I'll spend *all* my time designing their books, laying them out and getting them off to the printer?"

If this happened anywhere else, especially a "big" publishing house such as Random House or Simon & Schuster, the Editor-in-chief probably would have said, "Thanks, but no thanks." But some smaller houses (such as Career Press) probably would have taken the time to consider such a change in plans.

Whatever the outcome, Jinny, who was not *remotely* qualified for the opening as it was described and advertised, would have given herself a chance to actually get a job by getting the editor to *redefine the job so it fit her qualifications.*

In actual fact, it worked. She is a great employee!

It's okay to be a copycat

Feel free to "copy" typical interview questions *you* should expect to be asked and ask them of the interviewer instead:

What are the company's (department's) strengths and weaknesses?

What was the last great challenge faced by the department? How did you and your team handle it?

Can you tell me about a successful project and how you managed it?

Can you tell me about some recent problems you've faced and how you (as a team) overcame them?

What's your definition of success? What's your definition of failure?

If you could change one thing about the way this department works (or is structured or is managed or is compensated), what would it be?

How often do you and your team go out to *socialize* outside of work? Is such extracurricular activity actively promoted? Tolerated? Discouraged?

Ask for the job if you want it

The more sales-oriented the job—the more "Type A" the interviewer or the observed company culture—the more aggressively you need to "close" the sale. In fact, lack of real aggression in these situations will probably be reason enough *not* to offer you the job at all.

Is it okay to take notes?

I suspect I could find equal numbers of recruiters, executives, and interviewers to come down on either side of this question. Of course, it's okay for the *interviewer* to take notes, which is why I believe it is okay for the interviewee, too. Not just okay, but encouraged.

Why? There are a few good reasons:

You can't possibly remember everything...no matter how good your memory. And yet you certainly want to remember what *you* said, what *he* said, what seemed *right*, what felt *wrong*, titles, numbers...all the myriad things that went on during the interview. As long as you ask permission first, I believe taking notes is an absolute requirement if you want to accurately reconstruct what went on during an interview (or a series of interviews in a single day at the same company).

I believe many, if not most, interviewers, will interpret your note-taking as a sign of professionalism and seriousness, as long as you don't bring an iBook or Palm Pilot and keep your nose buried in it the entire time.

It is essential for your follow up. I am going to encourage you to write brief individual notes to every single person you meet on an interview, from the receptionist to the person who got your coffee, and even more targeted and longer letters to all the people with whom you actually interviewed. How can you be sure of the spelling of that many names, titles, etc. without good notes? How can you make sure to answer (again) the objection you know may be the key thing obstructing your hiring? How can you schmooze the colleague who seemed a little cold to your candidacy, perhaps jealous because *he* wanted (or expected) your job?

You may need to use your notes in the interview itself—jotting down a question you don't want to forget (while the interviewer drones on), a point you want to raise, an example you want to emphasize. This will allow you to bring up a point when it's the right time, which may be quite a while down the road, even at the very end of the interview.

You should walk in with notes—the questions you intend to ask, detailed notes on financials, specific points you want to remember, detailed data you want to incorporate in an answer or question. So getting the interviewer used to your "consulting my notes" makes it a lot easier to ask permission to take notes during the interview itself. But be careful. You don't want to appear to be constantly referring to your notes every time the interviewer asks a question:

"Where did you go to college, Jim?"

"Uh, just a minute, let me consult my notes."

Personally, I wouldn't want anything but an attractive notebook that is extracted from an equally professional looking attache case, along with a quality pen (not a disposable!). I find the use of a notebook computer much too distracting (as an interviewer), but it may be acceptable in high-tech industries where the interviewer could consider such technology a given (even a plus).

I'd never recommend a tape recorder, unless you plan to arrest the interviewer immediately after the interview. I see no positive value and a host of negative reactions to it.

Whatever you use, remember the point of the interview is to listen, then talk. Write as little as you need. And if you aren't very good at note-taking and listening at the same time (or taking notes while retaining eye contact), practice. No one wants to talk to your forehead.

Chapter 2

Questions TO ASK
YOURSELF

Who are you?

What are your strengths?

What is important to you?

What specific things do you require in the job you're seeking? Adventure, glamour, a bigger office, more money?

Where do want to work?

At what sized company?

With how many people under you?

What are your long-term goals?

What are your short-term goals?

What have you already done to accomplish the latter?

What do you still need to do?

Whew! And you were afraid the *interviewer* was going to ask tough questions!

There are plenty of questions to ask *yourself* long before you even think of letting your fingers wander through the want ads.

Answering these questions should enable you to define both short- and long-term goals—personal, professional, and financial—and could even help you develop a roadmap to reach those dreams. Additionally, they will help you better assess the "fit" between a company's culture, the job, the boss, and you. Unless you do this kind of analysis, on what basis will you be evaluating job offers?

As the old saying goes, if you don't know where you're going, any road will take you there.

So let's make a few lists to help you assess who you are, what's important to you, and what this analysis should tell you about the kind of company you want to work for. You'll quickly see that this is a far more detailed and completely different "assessment" than you were advised to do when collecting data for your resume.

Questions about you as a person

What are your key values?

What kinds of people do you enjoy spending time with?

Describe your personality.

What do you most like doing?

What do you least like doing?

Are you a risk-taker or risk averse?

What in your personal life causes you the most stress (relationships, money, time constraints, etc.)

What in your personal life gives you the most pleasure?

If you had to spend 40 hours a week doing a single activity, what would it be?

What were your favorite subjects in school? Would they still be your favorites today?

What were your strongest subjects?

What games and sports do you enjoy? What does the way you play them say about you?

Are you overly competitive? Do you give up too easily?

Are you a good loser or a bad winner? Do you rise to a challenge or back away?

What kinds of friends do you tend to have? Do you look for people who are just like you or who will laugh at all of your jokes? Do you tolerate differences? What has caused you to break up friendships? What does this say about you?

If you were to ask a group of friends and acquaintances to describe you, what adjectives would *they* use? Why do you think they would describe you in those terms? Are there specific behaviors, skills, achievements, or failures that caused them to choose those adjectives? What are they?

Questions about you as a professional

What kinds of people do you like working with? What kinds do you dislike working with?

What are your goals and aspirations?

What would it take to transform yourself into someone who's passionate about every workday?

What *are* your passions?

How can you make yourself more marketable in today's competitive job market?"

List your current strengths, abilities, and values

The following list of descriptive adjectives should help you further define who you really are, both professionally and personally. Check those words or phrases that you believe describe you, and keep them in mind when assessing any job offer or any company and its attendant culture.

____ Active

____ Active in sports

____ Active reader

____ Active volunteer

____ Adaptable

____ Adventurous

____ Ambitious

____ Artistic

____ Attractive

____ Brave/heroic

____ Calm

____ Computer literate

____ Confident

____ Courteous

____ Creative

____ Decisive

____ Dedicated

____ Detail-oriented

____ Directed

____ Dynamic

____ Economical

____ Empathetic

____ Ethical

____ Excellent analytical skills

____ Excellent math skills

____ Experienced

____ Extrovert

____ Flexible

____ Fluent in other languages

____ Focused

____ Goal-oriented

____ Good delegating skills

____ Good leadership skills

____ Good listener

____ Good mathematical skills

____ Good negotiating skills

____ Good oral

____ Good written
     communicator

____ Graceful

____ Handle stress well

____ Hardworking

____ High energy

____ Highly educated

____ Honest

____ Introvert

____ Learn from mistakes

____ Left-brained

____ Like people

____ Like to travel

____ Logical

____ Love animals

____ Love children

____ Loyal

____ Make friends easily

____ Moral

____ Musical

____ Neat

____ Obsessive

____ Organized

____ Passionate

____ Passive

____ Patient

____ Perfectionist

____ Performer

____ Physically strong

____ Precise

____ Professional

____ Quick-thinking

____ React well to
     authority

____ Religious

____ Responsible

____ Right-brained

____ Risk averse

____ Risk taker

____ Sales personality

____ Self-motivated

____ Sports fan

____ Strong-willed

____ Supportive of
     others

____ Tenacious

____ Welcome change

____ Well groomed

____ (Other) ____

These are all positive attributes, of one kind or another, to one company or another. After you've checked all of those you believe best describe you, ask your friends if they agree with your assessment—we aren't always the best judges of our own characters, are we?

You can use this list in a few important ways. First, it will help you better answer two key questions:

How do these positives match up with the qualities you believe are necessary for success in the job/career path you've chosen?

Do you have the qualities generally associated with the level of responsibility/job title you are seeking?

For example, if you are seeking a promotion to vice president at a major corporation, which would mean significant financial responsibility and hundreds of employees under your benevolent control, you will have a problem getting an interview, let alone the job, if you can't demonstrate managerial, team-building, motivational and financial skills and experience (among others). So if you lack all or most of those characteristics, your current goal isn't realistic and you must create a plan to attain the skills and experience, you need to reach your professional goals.

Another important question is suggested by this list:

How many of these qualities/abilities do you *want* to use in your job?

Alternately, how many of the qualities you've deemed most important to your sense of self do you need to involve in my job? Only you can figure this out, but I suspect most people would be happy if their jobs utilized *more* of their abilities and interests rather than *fewer.* I dare say the happiest people I've ever met are those able to employ the qualities, skills, and talents they deem important at a job that deems them equally important and a company at which *those specific attributes* lead to success.

Another way to utilize this list is to identify qualities you believe are important to your next job or your future career but that you lack. This will enable you to create a plan to develop, attain, or obtain what you want and need to succeed in your chosen path and reach your expressed goals.

What kind of life are you seeking?

How can you know what you want if you haven't taken the time to assess what's really important to you? Look at the following list of values (adapted from *Targeting the Job You Want,* one of an excellent series produced by The Five O'Clock Club, a top job-search group). Rate how important each is to you—1 for least important, 4 for very important:

Of those descriptions marked 4, identify the five *most* important to you right now. Then, of *those* five, admit which you would give up (if any) if you had to. Which would you *never* give up, no matter what?

Based on this exercise, you should be able to compose a brief paragraph describing the values of the company you'd (ideally) want to work for and the job you'd (ideally) love to have.

____ Adventure

____ Being considered an expert

____ Challenging tasks

____ Chance to advance

____ Chance to create

____ Chance to grow

____ Chance to have an impact

____ Chance to lead

____ Chance to learn

____ Chance to participate

____ Clear expectations

____ Clear procedures

____ Competition

____ Creativity

____ Enjoyable colleagues

____ Enjoyable surroundings

____ Enjoyable tasks

____ Excitement

____ Fast pace

____ Freedom from worry

____ Glamour

____ Having responsibility

The practical aspects of your job hunt

In addition to the kind of person you are, which will give you a better idea of the kind of people you want to work with and the environment in which you want to work, there are some more mundane questions you need to ask yourself:

❏ Where (geographically) do you want to work?

❏ Do you prefer a large city, small city, town or somewhere as far away from civilization as possible?

❏ Do you prefer a warm or cold climate?

❏ Do you prefer a large or small company? Define your terms (by sales, income, employees, etc.).

❏ What kinds of products/services/accounts would you prefer to work with?

❏ Do you mind traveling frequently? What percentage of your time do you consider "reasonable"?

❏ What salary would you like to receive?

❏ What's the *lowest* salary you'll accept?

❏ Are there any benefits (such as an expense account, medical and/or dental insurance, company car, etc.) you must or would like to have?

❏ Are you planning to attend graduate school at some point in the future? If so, is it important to you that a tuition reimbursement plan be part of the company benefits package?

❏ Is it important that the company have a formal employee-training program?

What can you learn from past jobs?

For each job you've held in the past, describe those factors that made one enjoyable, satisfying, or rewarding and another boring, frustrating, or just plain hell. Be as specific as possible. Consider everything from the company's location, the size of its (or your) offices, perks (or lack thereof), your subordinates and supervisors, responsibilities (or lack thereof), promotional opportunities, hours, benefits, etc.

____ Helping people

____ Helping society

____ Independence

____ Influencing people

____ Intellectual stimulation

____ Leadership

____ Meeting challenges

____ Money

____ Moral fulfillment

____ Personal growth

____ Power

____ Prestige

____ Public contact

____ Recognition from peers

____ Recognition from society

____ Recognition from superiors

____ Slow pace

____ Stability (security)

____ Structure

____ Time with family

____ Working alone

____ Working for something you believe in

____ Working on a team

The more comprehensive you make this analysis, the more easily you will begin to notice behavioral patterns. This exercise may help you hone in on a particular requirement (a corner office), something to avoid at all costs (a boss who's passive-aggressive), or even some aspect of your own personality that you need to work on (lamenting a lack of promotional opportunities when you've never stayed at any job longer than six months).

What can you learn from past bosses?

How well do you interact with authority figures—bosses, teachers, parents?

Even if every other aspect of a job is wonderful, you could be dying to move on just because you hate your boss. Hey, it happens. So before you extract yourself from the frying pan and deposit yourself directly into the fire, you might want to do the following exercise as well: Make a list of every boss you've ever had, using the broadest possible definition of "boss." Divide them into three lists: those with whom you *never* had a problem, those with whom you had *some* problems, and those with whom you *always* seemed to have problems.

After you've developed these three lists, try to identify the common factors that would explain the problems you had with the third group. Were they all old, married white men who smoked cigars? Were they all fast-charging sales types? Were they all bosses for the same kinds of companies (large, small, whatever)?

You get the idea. The more you know about the kinds of bosses under whom you thrived and those beneath whom you withered, the better chance you have of finding the right fit the next time around.

I'll use myself (again) as an example: One of my early jobs in magazine publishing was as an advertising sales representative for a trade magazine. I was ambitious, passionate, and a very good salesperson. After teaching me about the basics of ad sales, my boss pretty much kept out of the way and let me run. Boy, did I run! I set a single-year sales record that, I've been told, still stands.

Now, I didn't exactly do everything by the book. In fact, I threw the book away. I ignored *all* requests to do memos or reports or anything that would have taken time away from making sales (that is, making *me* more money). I did not communicate, I did not summarize, I did not report. I just sold. After a short time, my boss simply stopped asking for that stuff and decided to revel in the big jump his own income was taking due to my unbridled efforts.

I did so well that I got promoted to a bigger magazine, becoming the youngest sales manager in that company's history. My old boss went to my new boss and sang my praises. But he also told her, in virtually these terms, to just "let him the ___ alone. He's a maverick and won't follow any of your rules. He will make you a fortune, but he doesn't need to learn anything from you. Just let him sell and motivate his salespeople to sell."

Well, my new boss wasn't nearly as flexible as my old boss had been (nor, obviously, as bright). Instead of taking the recommended "hands-off" attitude, she wasted days of my time in a series of meetings explaining "how we do things at *this* magazine." It was a disaster from the gitgo, and it wasn't long before it was made pretty clear (by the VP of sales) that one of us was not going to be left standing.

A tremendous opportunity to move up to publisher of a major consumer travel publication materialized, as if on command. It represented a huge jump in responsibility and an equally huge jump in money. The only downside was that if I wanted the job, I would have to move to the Midwest—and I and my wife were confirmed New Yorkers. Plus, of course, she had a job she loved and informed me in no uncertain terms that she didn't intend to sacrifice her career for mine. (Good for her!) If my new boss had simply followed my first boss's advice, I probably would have turned the job down and continued on my well-planned rise at that trade publisher.

Well, she didn't. So I had little choice. Luckily, my wife's boss found a way for her to keep her job...and do it from the Midwest. So we moved. While the situation looked fantastic, it turned out to be a company in well-hidden trouble with *two* control-freak bosses (a husband and wife, no less) to whom I reported. Within 10 months, I was looking for a job again...and making the move back to the New York area...where no one wanted to particularly give me a job approaching the money or responsibility I had just had!

The result was a company called Career Press, which I founded not long thereafter, using my severance check from the Midwest. Nearly 20 years later, it is a well-known publisher of 72 non-fiction books a year—including, of course, this one!

Now, I am not at all unhappy that things worked out the way they did. I became my own boss and have absolutely never regretted the unexpected path my career took. But it wasn't exactly a free choice, was it? It started with a *promotion*, of all things. Did I ask *anything* about that new boss? How compatible we were? Her style of management? Did I talk to anyone else that had worked for her? Did I talk to my predecessor in that position?

NO.

Did I ask about the salary and bonuses and special deals. Oh, you betcha I did.

Getting the message?

It gets worse. Because I was in an untenable situation, the Midwest job looked like a godsend. Well, did I ask *anything* about my two new bosses before starting to pack? How compatible we were? Their (absolutely contradictory) styles of management? Did I talk to anyone else that had worked for them? Did I talk to my predecessor in that position?

You know the answers, right?

I do not handle authority well—a surprise, I'm sure. I guess I knew that in my heart. But I never took the time to really analyze myself enough to discover how essential that part of my nature really was. Even after it caused one meltdown, I walked right into a second.

A single aspect of *your* personality can have a similar affect on your relationship with a boss or company. Take the time to know yourself well enough to at least anticipate a problem!

Don't wear sandals at a white-shoe company

Birds of a feather *do* flock together. And different companies tend to attract particular "species" of employees. A company's physical environment, management attitude, policies, and the personality of the "birds" that predominate comprise the company's corporate culture. Is it a "loose" atmosphere with jean-clad creative types running amok? Or a buttoned-down, blue-suited autocracy with a long list of rules to follow. . . during timed coffee breaks?

Companies are sometimes dominated by a single personality—a still-active founder or an executive who has exerted a strong, long-lasting influence on policies and style. Think Jack Welch at GE, Bill Gates at Microsoft, or Larry Ellison at Oracle. While there are exceptions, such companies tend to be "closely held" fiefdoms whose every level reflects the "cult of personality." If that personality is a despot, benign or otherwise, even a decentralized management structure won't create a company everyone wants to work for. (Gates, for one, is reportedly a very difficult boss.)

Family-owned companies often pose similar problems. Your chances to make decisions and take responsibility may be tied to your last name. Barely competent family members may wind up with cushy jobs and high pay, while you and other "outsiders" do all the work. While many such firms are privately held, even publicly traded companies in which family members hold a significant block of stock (such as Ford or, again, Microsoft) still answer primarily to the family.

Many larger, more decentralized companies will spread decision-making power and opportunities for advancement somewhat more evenly. However, such companies often encourage to compete with each other rather than to direct their collective energies against competing organizations.

If managers regularly spend half their time politicking or writing self-serving memos to the boss, it's a survival-of-the-fittest (or survival-of-tne-best-memo-writer) atmosphere. People attuned to corporate in-fighting might relish such a company; those who just want to do their jobs and be rewarded for their work will find it an unfriendly place to work.

Some companies are bursting with energy. Their offices seem to reverberate with a steady hum of activity. Such a high-key environment is right for aggressive go-getters who are unafraid of such a fast pace and more than ready, even eager, to jump into the fray. Other workplaces are calmer, quiet, almost studious in nature. Such low-key firms are probably better choices for more laid-back personalities.

While a high-energy or low-key atmosphere says little about a particular company's chances for success, it may have much to do with your own on-the-job performance, success, and happiness. Matching dissimilar corporate and individual personalities usually results in a new job search.

If you run across a company that seems to give off no signals at all, beware! This is usually the direction-less organization, one that lacks both an agenda and dynamic leadership. Without such leadership, you can be certain that this organization will flounder, usually when things start going wrong and the timely implementation of company-wide decisions is required.

Clearly, the more you know about the companies you're considering, the better off you'll be. For those of you—and that should be *all* of you—who want to research a specific company and/or job description, Chapter 3 will give you the necessary hints and resources.

Once you've analyzed yourself and investigated a targeted company's culture, a simple but extremely important question should come to mind:

How does your self-description match that of the culture at the company you're thinking of joining?

If you are laid back and not particularly driven to overachieve, a company that describes itself as "hard-charging" may not be for you, even if you can actually convince them to hire you given that description.

The Gallup Organization is a unique example of corporate culture. When my good friend Tony Rutigliano was recruited by them, their offer was so enticing that it seemed like a "no-brainer"...until Tony asked about exactly what he'd be doing, his job title, and to whom he'd be reporting.

"Well," the recruiter confided, "we work a little differently here. We expect that you'll wander around for a while, maybe a few months, and then *you'll* tell *us* what you really want to do. We don't really have formal job descriptions. And you can use any reasonable title."

Needless to say, Tony, a veteran of a number of traditional magazine publishing companies, was a bit taken aback. Wander around? Create his own job description?

Since Tony was a bit of an entrepreneur at heart and a confident bloke to boot, he decided to give it a try. Some years later, he is not just fantastically successful, he is completely happy. Gallup's corporate culture, as unusual as it was, turned out to be a great fit for him.

Would it have been an equally rewarding and ultimately successful move for you? Not if you were someone who expected or required a rigid organizational chart. Anyone too uncomfortable to just "wander about" would probably have run for the hills after a couple of days (presuming they were crazy enough to take the job in the first place).

There may be nothing inherently wrong with an organization you're considering—it just might be a horrible fit *for you* and throw you completely off the career track you have outlined. Maybe you will survive, maybe you will thrive, maybe you will find yourself looking for another job in six months, maybe it will cause you to positively change your goals. In any event, you must know what you're getting into and do everything you can to prepare for that environment.

The importance of goals

I've mentioned the importance of goals a little already. Now it's time to emphasize them. Short- and long-term goal-setting must become a habit. Once a year, reevaluate not just the progress you're making toward your long-term goals, but whether they need to be tweaked, heavily modified, or even changed completely. Life is not static. Neither are your goals—they will (and should) change with circumstance, age, position, etc.

Remember that setting goals will not only help you define where you want to go, but what you need to get there. If you have decided that you eventually want to be Chief Financial Officer of a large corporation, you may well need an MBA or similar graduate degree. When do you plan to get it? Full or part-time? If the latter, will the company allow a modified schedule so you can go to school while you work? Is there a tuition reimbursement plan? Is there already a program in place to which you can apply? Your goals and your estimation of what you need to do and be to reach them will greatly influence the questions you ask.

It's equally important to make your goals realistic. There is nothing wrong with reaching for the stars, providing you have the appropriate step stool. If you aren't a high school graduate, you *can* aspire to becoming chairman of IBM, but your short-term goals better include some serious additional education! If you want to be a prize-winning author, passing a creative writing class might be a nice first step. Goals are realistic if there is a clear-cut path that you can follow to reach them. It may be a hard and long road, but if you truly believe you can actually reach its end with sufficient effort, then the goal is realistic.

Even if a goal is completely unrealistic, I would not necessarily counsel you to drop it. First of all, who's to say it really *is* unrealistic? You may have little or no natural writing ability and couldn't draw a straight line if your life depended on it. Would I be willing to bet you probably *won't* become the creative director of one of the world's top three advertising agencies. Well, I'm a betting man, so I probably *would* take that bet. But the human spirit is an amazing thing. Who says with the right education, jobs, and practice that your goal, though unrealistic, couldn't be realized? And even if it weren't, the additional educational and dedication certainly wouldn't hurt your career prospects!

What if the goal is realistic but you are simply unwilling or unable to do what's necessary to reach it? Change it. Why kid yourself? While luck plays a factor in many careers, it is certainly not the only factor—the one common denominator of virtually any success story is hard work. If you aren't willing to work hard, almost *any* goal may be unrealistic.

Your immediate and future personal/financial goals will, of course, have a great affect on your decision-making and on the questions you ask (and answers you absolutely need to know). If you're unmarried and childless and someone actually offers to pay you to wander the globe, you may be more than alright with the arrangement. But what if you anticipate getting married or having kids in a year or two? What if you know you have to prepare to take care of an older relative? Your financial needs may dramatically change. The kind of hours, travel, etc. you're willing to take on now may need to be radically overhauled. You may not mind relocating once a year *now*, but resist relocating at all after you've "settle down." If you have chosen a job/career/industry/company in which declining to relocate may mean the *end* of your job/career, your future plans must be part of your current equation.

Show me the money!

What is your current standard of living, and are you happy with it?

Can you comfortably afford your current lifestyle, or are you living beyond your means with nothing in the bank and a fistful of maxed-out credit cards?

What standard of living do you aspire to in two years? Five years? 10 years?

What salary (or package) is required to meet these targets?

Besides salary, what benefits or package components do you consider essential? Nice? Unnecessary?

Answering these questions is obviously important. You have to realistically define your financial wants and needs. How can you know how much you need if you can't figure out how to live on what you've got right now? Develop a budget. Develop a financial plan.

As you analyze the cost of some of your long-range planning, you're going to shock yourself, maybe even presume you'd better give up right now. Especially if you are a recent college graduate, laying out what "life" costs could be daunting. But don't forget to look at the other side of the coin: what you're going to earn. Even if your starting salary were $25,000 and you never got a better job or a raise (and leaving out the "costs" of inflation, which is just a pain in the butt anyway), if you work for

40 years (sounds wonderful when I put it that way, doesn't it?), you'll earn $1 million. Earn, on average, $50,000 a year—$2 million. And if you quickly ascend to that $100,000 a year level? That's right—$4 million or more.

If you are (hopefully) given the choice between two or more jobs, you need some basis upon which to decide between them. If one job pays substantially less than the other, but is much closer to your "ideal" career path, has more promise, etc., you really need to know whether you can afford to take it...because you very much might *want* to take it, despite the lower pay.

You need to look farther into the future than tomorrow. Companies still do survive and thrive, and a company you're considering (especially if it is a non-high-tech behemoth that's been a Fortune 500 company for decades) may very well be around, and doing quite well, when your grandkids are reading this book. What does this mean in terms of your job hunt? Your financial prospects at that firm two, five, or even 10 years in the future may be very relevant indeed. Taking a position that pays less than you would prefer at a company where you believe (based on your research, conversations, maybe even promises from the interviewer) your financial goals could well be reached or even exceeded farther down the line may be a smart move. And the bigger the company, the more likely there will be significant opportunities to change jobs, even areas (hence, careers) without leaving the company.

What if you are offered more, perhaps *substantially* more, rather than less? Simple question: What will you earn if you're fired or quit after a month, or three or six? Isn't that a reality you need to at least consider?

And if you are let go after a month, was it the right move?

If you choose a job purely because it pays substantially more—and the job (or the company!) disappears after a month, or two or three—what have you actually made? A heck of a lot less than you thought you were getting! Suddenly a $12,000 annual difference becomes a difference of $3,000, $2,000, or even $1,000. Not to mention that you are now out of a job. How much are you losing while you find another job? Yep. More than the $12,000 on which your supposedly well-thought-out decision was based.

There's more to life than money, and money is only one aspect to consider about a job offer. Make sure you know enough about who you are, where you want to go, what you need, and what you want so you're ready to make an *informed* decision, not just a pure comparison of dollars and cents.

This is not your grandfather's job market (or, for that matter, your mother's). There is no security. Do you remember (or have you heard about) those ancient days when you took a job and could count on reasonable raises for 40 years or so until you retired with your gold watch? We aren't in Kansas anymore. Those days are long gone, so making a decision to take a job that does not really fulfill your long-term goals (maybe not even many of your short-term goals) just because it pays more money (even a lot more money) is not necessarily smart.

Interestingly, keeping money in this kind of perspective ties in nicely with the Five o'clock Club's notion of creating a "40-year vision" of your career. If you read any of the books by its founder, Kate Wendleton—and I suggest you read all of them; they're the best set of job search books on the market—you will see how often her members choose between three, five, or more offers and wind up taking the one that pays the least in the short run. This is not because each of them has decided that money is not as important as some of the other factors we've been discussing. In many cases, it's because they had a clear vision of the financial potential of each offer down the road and made a more long-term decision.

Besides, I doubt there are many people, who, on their deathbeds, fervently proclaimed, " I just wish I had worked harder" or "I just wish I had made another sale." Always give personal goals the same weight as career/professional goals unless you have consciously decided to do otherwise. Most of us don't consciously decide anything of the sort, we just let the professional goals overwhelm the personal. We "become our jobs." This is not inherently a bad thing, but it's not good if it throws the rest of our lives completely out of balance.

Be careful how many of your decisions in life, including, of course, where you work, are based solely on money. The older I get, the more I see how many of the decisions I've had to make have been based far too much on money (either wanting or not having) and not nearly enough on conscious lifestyle choices. I feel sometimes, and I suspect many of you do too, that money makes a mockery of the term "choices"— What do you mean, choices? A man's gotta do what a man can afford (or not).

Not to get into a Dennis Miller rant here, but if money isn't the root of all evil, it can certainly be considered the root of one heck of a lot of dissatisfaction. There are, at the risk of sounding simplistic, plenty of people without what many of us would consider "a lot of money" (define with your own number of zeros) who are quite content in their lives, thank you very much. And of course there are the plethora of "poor little rich kids" who seem to have received nothing but grief with their inherited zillions. So keep money in its place. It's important, even essential, but it ain't all there is.

Are you moving too fast?

Don't be too ready to give up what you already have—your current job—just because you believe the grass just has to be greener "over there." Ask yourself some smart questions first:

Can you achieve your ultimate career path in your current company?

How does your current job differ from your ideal job?

What specific skills and experience do you need to transform one into the other?

How can you transfer skills you already have to a completely different career?

How would you describe your absolute dream job? Where would you be? What would you be doing? Who would you be working with/for? What would you be earning?

What additional education or training would you need to achieve this dream job? If you obtained the education or

training but *didn't* attain the dream job, how do you think your current job or career path would be affected?

You may be putting the cart before the horse if you're already gung-ho on interviewing at other companies but haven't asked yourself these important questions. You already have (one hopes) a good reputation at your current job—a good history, friends, experience, respect. If all of that is true, you should want to move on only if your answers to the previous questions were negative.

If there is *any* way to stay at your current job and/or at your current company if the answers are *positive*, think long and hard about why you would want to make a change. My advice would be to evaluate what you would need to do to create your "ideal job" *at your current company*, even if you hate your current job, current boss, or current situation. First, analyze what it would take to make you happy. And if you can fathom *any* way to do it without going through the job-search process, do so. It's a jungle out there, and better the frying pan you're already in than throwing yourself upon someone else's pyre.

Of course, this is a moot point if, having done the analysis, you conclude there is simply no viable way to get even remotely close to your ideal job at a compensation level that you need. Or if the very nature of the company (few employees, a field you want out of completely, etc.) makes it moot.

But don't be afraid to ask the questions raised at the beginning of this section and, perhaps, two more:

Are there any training programs available that may make the kind of move you want possible?

Presuming there *is* "room at the top," what specifically do you think you would have to do to earn the job title/salary/responsibilities, etc. you want (the ones you're willing to search for elsewhere)? *Can* you do it? Within a timeframe you deem reasonable?

By taking a more patient approach, you may give yourself the best of both possible worlds—working towards your goals at your *present* company while still "testing the waters" at others.

I hope by the time you finish the exercises in this chapter, you are more than ready to sit down and describe not just the companies you'd like to work for, but your duties and responsibilities, your new boss's personality, the people you will be working with, and where you'd like to be two, five, 10,...yes, even 40 years down the road. If you have honestly and completely answered the questions you asked of yourself, I think you will be ready to do just that.

Chapter 3

Questions TO ASK
During YOUR RESEARCH

Research is an essential first step in any job search. If you know nothing about the firm, department, job, or boss, you have no real clue of how to "position" your answers to any of the interviewer's questions (or "target" your own questions). That's why you can't just go in with a bunch of basic questions that you could have easily answered yourself at the library or online.

You have many skills and qualifications and talents, some or all of which may be pertinent. *One* of which may be key. How do you know? You won't.

So the research is not just to give you a set of questions to ask. It's to help you customize those questions and target your answers to the interviewer's questions.

Here's a complete list of the facts you should know about each company at which you schedule an interview:

The Basics

☐ Directions to the office you're visiting.

☐ Headquarters location (if different).

- ❏ Some idea of domestic and international branches.

- ❏ Relative size (compared to other companies in the field).

- ❏ Annual billings, sales, and/or income (last two years).

- ❏ Subsidiary companies; specialized divisions.

- ❏ Departments (overall structure).

- ❏ Major accounts, products, or services.

- ❏ Major competitors.

The Not-so-basics

- ❏ History of the firm (specialties, honors, awards, famous names).

- ❏ Names, titles, and backgrounds of top management.

- ❏ Existence (and type) of training program.

- ❏ Relocation policy.

- ❏ Relative salaries (compared to other companies in field or by size).

- ❏ Recent developments concerning the company and its products or services.

- ❏ Everything you can learn about the career, likes and dislikes of the person(s) that are interviewing you.

Where to start looking

For a very broad overview of any industry, consult the U.S. Bureau of Labor Statistics (http://stats.bls.gov) which uses business and economic trends and changing demographics to chart expected growth in employment for occupations in every industry over a 10-year period. The most current edition of the *Occupational Outlook Handbook* (2002-03 ed.) is available here, as are online quarterly updates, a wealth of industry and economic information, and the most current (2002-03) edition of *The Career Guide to Industries*, the companion to the *OOH*.

In addition, here's a core list of research sources, many of which should be available in your local library:

❑ The *Encyclopedia of Business Information Sources* lists some 25,000 sources on more than a thousand specific subjects, including directories, associations, and more. The bi-annual *Directories in Print* organizes companies by industry. The annual *Job Seekers Guide to Public and Private Companies* covers 25,000 companies, with detailed information on specific job titles and openings for each. (All from Gale Research Inc.)

❑ *Directory of Corporate Affiliations* and *Directory of Leading Private Companies* (Reed Reference Publishing, New Providence, NJ 07974).

❑ Dun and Bradstreet's family of corporate reference resources: the *Million Dollar Directory* (160,000 companies with a net worth of more than $500,000), *Top 50,000 Companies* (those with a minimum net worth of just under $2 million) and *Business Rankings* (details on the nation's top 7,500 firms). Another volume— *Reference Book of Corporate Managements/ America's Corporate Leaders*—provides detailed biographical data on the principal officers and directors of some 12,000 corporations. (Who says you can't find out about the quirks and hobbies of your interviewer?) All of these volumes are available in most libraries or from Dun's Marketing Services (3 Sylvan Way, Parsippany, NJ 07054).

❑ *Moody's Industry Review* (available from Moody's Investors Service, Inc., 99 Church St., New York, NY 10007).

❑ *Standard and Poors' Register of Corporations, Directors and Executives* includes corporate listings for more than 45,000 firms and 72,000 biographical listings (available from Standard and Poors, 25 Broadway, New York, NY 10004).

❑ *Thomas's Register of American Manufacturers* (Thomas Publishing Company, 1 Penn Plaza, New York, NY 10110). Annual profile of more than 150,000 manufacturers. Features information on primary products and services plus more than 100,000 trade and brand names.

❑ *Ward's Business Directory,* a four-volume reference work that includes listings of nearly 100,000 companies, the majority of them privately held, and details that are usually most difficult to acquire about such firms, such as number of employees, annual sales, etc. (Gale Research Inc.).

❏ The *Standard Directory of Advertisers* (also known as the Advertiser Red Book, because of its bright red cover) lists more than 17,000 companies that commit some portion of their budgets to advertising and promotion. It is available in two editions—classified and geographical. Major product lines and the agencies to whom they are assigned are listed, as well as names and job functions of key marketing personnel at the listed companies and their agencies.

❏ *The Fortune 500* is an annual compilation by *Fortune* magazine of the top U.S. businesses, ranked by sales. It will become particularly important later in your search, when you're targeting specific companies. At that time, it will enable you to analyze not only where a particular company ranks in the overall U.S. economy, but also whether it is falling or on the rise, and how it measures up against other companies in its field.

Two other potential sources of leads include *The Oxbridge Directory of Newsletters* (check your library), a listing of thousands of newsletters in a range of industries, and the *Professional Exhibits Directory* (Gale Research Inc.), which lists more than 2,000 trade shows and conventions. Why not consider attending some to learn more about the companies and products out there?

Become acquainted with a key reference resource—the various volumes of the *Standard Rate and Data Service* (SRDS), all of which are available in most libraries. The volume in which you're interested is Business Publications. In it you'll find a list, by industry, of the thousands of business (or trade) magazines currently being published.

These publications are prime sources of information, especially if you are relatively new to the job market. Start reading them regularly (many are collected in metropolitan public libraries). Write for recent issues of the leading publications for the fields you've targeted. If you make reading a weekly practice, you will accomplish a number of important goals. You'll begin to absorb information about:

- ❑ The industry as a whole.

- ❑ Major companies in the field.

- ❑ Trends, new products, and the general outlook for specific product categories.

- ❑ Major players in the industry—both companies and individuals.

- ❑ Industry/professional jargon or "buzzwords."

In addition, published interviews with leading practitioners in the field will give you insight on how they approach their specific jobs.

Finally, there are the major magazines you should turn to now and then to complete your research: *The Wall Street Journal, Barron's, Business Week, Fortune, Forbes, Industry Week, Nation's Business, National Business Employment Weekly,* and *Inc.,* as well as the pertinent trade magazines in your field.

Finding information on smaller companies

A majority of new jobs are created by small companies, but you may not learn much about them in the standard reference resources previously listed. If your initial research proves fruitless or only marginally productive, try the following outside sources of information:

- ❐ **The chamber of commerce** in the community that's home to the company or division. You can find out how the company has been performing. Has it been growing or shrinking? How many people does it employ? How many did it employ in the community two years ago? Do people consider it a good place to work?

- ❐ **Business/industry associations:** Many trade associations are excellent resources for industry data and statistics as well as general employment trends and specific opportunities. Four good resources are the *Encyclopedia of Associations* and *Business Organizations, Agencies and Publications Directory* (both from Gale Research Inc.), *National Trade and Professional Associations of the United States* (Columbia Books, Inc.) and the *Association Yellow Pages* (Monitor Publishing Co.).

- ❐ **Executive, professional, and technical placement agencies:** If you are getting the job interview through an agency, see how much you can learn about the prospective employer from them (and see Chapter 4).

❏ **Business editors:** Turn the tables on the news media: Ask *them* the questions! A community newspaper's business reporter or editor will usually be the person most knowledgeable about local companies. They'll know about developments at particular companies, how employees like working for them, and their reputations in the community.

❏ **Trade magazines:** Every industry has at least one trade magazine covering its developments. Call a junior (assistant or associate) editor. Ask if the publication has covered the company and if you can obtain copies of the article(s).

❏ **School alumni:** A college placement office, your fraternity/sorority, or alumni association might be able to tell you about someone working at the company. Alumni are usually happy to help someone from their alma mater.

❏ **Stockbrokers/analysts:** If the company is public, it will have an investor relations representative who can tell you which brokers and analysts "follow the stock." This means that a representative of the brokerage firm has visited with the company, written a detailed report for investors, and analyzed its industry, balance sheet, and management. Call the broker and ask for a copy of the report. It will be objective, very revealing, and give you terrific material with which to impress the interviewer.

❏ **Online:** There are a multitude of bulletin boards, databases, and discussion groups through which you can track down obscure information to impress a prospective employer in an interview. Your first step, of course, should be to check out the company's Website.

Here's a solid list of Websites to check out. Most are for research; some are just for advice; only one (the first) is hosted by a resume-writing service (and that's because of the excellent links the site offers):

1stresumes.com

6figurejobs.com

Acinet.org (America's Career Infonet, sponsored by the U.S. Dept. of Labor)

Ajb.dni.us (America's job bank)

Alumni-network.com (Hi-tech jobs)

Asktheemployer.com (a mentoring site)

Bestjobsusa.com

Bilingual-jobs.com

Bizjournals.com (Local business news from cities throughout the U.S.)

Businessweek.com

Businesswire.com

Career.com

Careerbuilder.com

Careerbuzz.com (hip and happening but for young people only)

Careerjournal.com (a Wall Street Journal company)

Careermag.com

Careermosaic.com

Careers.org (with 4,000 links to other sites)

Careershop.com

Computerjobs.com

Cyberkingemployment.com (56 languages, 130 countries)

Dice.com (primarily technical careers)

Dnb.com (info on 10,000,000 U.S. companies from Dun and Bradstreet)

Employment911.com

Elibrary.com (a research site with near-instant access to 13,000,000 magazine and newspaper articles)

Eresumes.com

Fiveoclockclub.com (one of the best "job hunt" sites)

Forbes.com

Hirediversity.com (if you're disabled)

Hoovers.com (good for company research)

Jobbankusa.com

Joblynx.com

Jobsearchengine.com (a meta site)

Jobstar.org

Jobtrak.com (primarily for college students; now part of Monster.com)

Jobweb.com (college students)

Latpro.com (if you're fluent in Spanish or Portuguese)

Monster.com

Myjobsearch.com (a meta site)

Nationjob.com

Nettemps.com (temp jobs)

Prnewswire.com (news on companies and individuals)

Recruitersonline.com (more than 2,000 registered recruiters)

Reuters.com

Truecareers.com

Vault.com

Wageweb.com (salary info)

Wetfeet.com (though most of their insider guides are way overpriced)

Worktree.com

Wsj.com (Wall Street Journal)

Note: Hotjobs.com is now part of Yahoo.

Vault.com

This site deserves special mention. Go to their message boards (the Electronic Water Cooler)—organized by industry, company, university, law school, business school, even career topic. The day I last checked, there were 883,132 messages listed (some quite old, but nevertheless, impressive). Talk about getting the inside scoop! There was a message from an employee at a major bank lamenting the size of their Christmas bonuses. Another from a major computer company (okay, *the* major computer company) giving pretty specific details about layoffs that hadn't been announced publicly. What a potential treasure trove of information!

Ask the company itself

Once you've culled the *outside*—and probably more objective—sources of information, take a look at what the company tells the public about itself. Check out the company's Website and/or call the company's Investor Relations or Human Resources departments to obtain the following:

❑ **Annual reports.** Mark Twain said that there are three kinds of lies—"lies, damned lies, and statistics"—and you'll find all of them in most annual reports. Read between the lines of the annual report to learn as much as you can about the company.

You will be able to tell how the company's sales and profits have been increasing or decreasing over the past few years, what its plans are for the years ahead and the health of the industry in which it operates.

In addition, an annual report should indicate how the company feels about its employees. Note whether the report features accomplishments of particular employees.

Does it have photos of people at work? Or does it stick strictly to "the numbers" and highlight the self-aggrandizing musings of the chairman?

❏ **Employee handbooks.** Be gutsy: Ask the company to send you a copy of this valuable document. At the very least, the handbook will tell you about benefits, vacation time, salary review policies, and other information you might not want to ask about in an initial interview. It also should give you valuable insights into the company's attitude toward its employees. Is in-house training provided? Is the company picnic a much-anticipated annual event?

❏ **Sales/marketing brochures.** Knowing about a company's products will help you determine whether you'd like to work for the organization and furnish great material upon which to base your questions.

❏ **Company newsletters.** There may be far more details about the company picnic than you would like, but there also might be some personal information about your interviewer, your future coworkers, or your future boss. You'll also get a better feel for how the company communicates with "the troops," how they view their future, new product launches, recent awards, etc., etc.

Although nobody enjoys doing it, homework does have its payoffs, especially during a job hunt. From the research you doggedly pursued on prospective employers, you should have learned several important things about each:

- ❏ What it's looking for in its employees.

- ❏ Its key products and markets.

- ❏ Whether it's hired employees from your school and how they've fared.

- ❏ Who the hiring manager is and what type of people he usually hires.

- ❏ Why you might enjoy working for that company.

All of this information will prove invaluable to you, not only during the interview, but in helping you get the interview in the first place.

Research from books, the Net, phone calls, interviews, etc., is all necessary, but don't disbelieve what your eyes and ears tell you. When you're waiting in reception, look and listen. What do the people seem like? Is it a loose atmosphere? Fast? Slow? Is there a lot of joking around? Or does every person who passes by look as if a well-loved pet just died? Are they even talking to each other? Or are they a row of Dilbert clones chained to their cubbyholes?

Plan to get to every interview early, and play a little detective. Talk to everyone you meet: What do you do? How long have you worked here? Do you like it?

Chapter 4

Questions TO ASK "Pre-INTERVIEWERS"

The questions provided in this chapter are those to *ask of anyone who lacks the final authority to hire you.* If you're relatively young and inexperienced, you may do a series of *informational interviews* to learn about an industry, company, or job you think you'd like. Depending on your level of experience, you may utilize an employment agency, recruiting firm, or headhunter. And even if you know you should do everything to avoid them, you may find yourself interviewing, on the phone or in person, with a Human Resources staffer.

None of these people can offer you a job. But all of them can offer you something almost as valuable: the information about the company, position, and hiring manager you *do* need to land that job.

This chapter will show you how to utilize each of these "pre-interviewers" and which questions to ask them.

Information please

An *informational interview* should be utilized by someone either new to the job market (for example, a recent high school or college graduate) or an experienced worker seeking a career change.

There is a huge difference between a job interview and an informational interview. In an informational interview, your goal is to learn as much as possible about the industry, company, and job you've targeted (although such an interview may come very early in the job-search process, long before you've begun to pursue specific companies or even a specific industry). If you are actively seeking a job at a specific company, such an interview is rarely one you would schedule at that company; rather, you should seek out a similar company in the same industry.

If you are more concerned with learning about a particular job description, not as picky about the industry, and not ready to hone in on specific companies, then you could seek an informational interview with someone in the same position at virtually *any* company in *any* industry.

A meeting with someone already doing what you soon *hope* to be doing is, by far, the best way to find out what you need to know *before* a formal job interview. You'll find that most people are happy to talk about their jobs. I know I often sit down with "friends of friends" and share what I've learned about book publishing. Because there is no immediate pressure on me to evaluate that "friend" as a candidate, I can be more informal, forthcoming, and relaxed.

You may learn of a specific job opening during an informational interview. If so, you are in an enviable position to unearth many important details about it. You may learn the identity of the actual interviewer (or, more important, the decision-maker) and, if you're lucky, something about her experience, values, and personality. With your contact's permission, you may even be able to use his name as a referral.

As you prepare to conduct informational interviews, there are, ideally, six individual goals you hope to fulfill during each:

1. To unearth current information about the industry, company, and pertinent job functions. *Remember:* Gaining knowledge and understanding of broad industry trends, the financial health of the industry and its key players, hiring opportunities, and the competitive picture are key components in your search for the right job.

2. To investigate each company's hiring policies: Who makes the decisions? Who are the key players? Is there a hiring season?

3. To sell yourself and leave a calling card: your resume.

4. To seek out advice to help you refine your job search.

5. To obtain referrals to expand your network of contacts.

6. To develop a list of follow-up activities that will heighten your visibility among your key contacts.

Of course, the line between the people who can give you information about a certain field you've targeted and potential employers in that field can sometimes blur. Don't be concerned—you'll soon learn when (and how) to shift the focus from interview*er* to interview*ee*.

> *To simplify this process, follow a single rule*: Show interest in the industry or job area under discussion, but never aggressively seek out information about particular openings—wait until the interviewer raises the possibility of your working there.

You may be surprised at how often the person you're interviewing turns to you and asks, "Would you be interested in _____ (a current job opening)?" If you *would* be interested in the position under discussion, by all means make your feelings known.

Smart Questions for an informational interview

In addition to any questions your research failed to answer (which, of course, you should ask now), here are some other smart questions to ask during any informational interview:

What are your duties and responsibilities?

How do you spend your day?

How did you get started at this company (or in your profession)?

What do you like most about your job? What do you like least?

What kind of person do you think is right for this kind of work?

What skills are in short supply here? (Careful: This is bordering on the aggressive!)

How can I learn more about this field? Are there specific trade journals I should be reading or associations I can join?

How can I meet others in this field?

What is the best way to get started (in this field or at this company)?

This is a question for recent graduates to ask.

I'm trying to get in to see people at some other organizations. Do you know anyone at these companies? May I use your name?

Given my credentials, where would you see me fitting in at a company like yours

This is probably as close to a "closing" question as you want in an informational interview. At worst, you'll get some valuable advice. At best, you may just get yourself a real interview.

Can you direct me to others in your department/organization/division/company with whom you think it would be appropriate for me to talk or meet?

Now it's possible that the interviewer will direct you to another person or two for the express purpose of educating you. After all, that *is* what you said you were there for. But there is another positive possibility: You may have impressed him. In fact, despite your assertion that you're "just seeking information," he may be thinking, "Hmmm, this guy is good. He may be right for that opening in Josh's department." In which case, you have just transformed an informational interview into a job interview...just by asking this single question. That's why I like it!

Questions for recruiters, headhunters, and employment agencies

Of the many outside counselors who can help you with your job search or arm you with job leads, employment agencies are on the bottom rung of the ladder. Dozens of them may get the same job openings from the same companies at the same time. Candidates are a bit like fast-food: First come, first served.

Recruiters are a decided step up, although not all of them work on an exclusive basis. So, again, there may be more than one or two of them seeking similar candidates for the same openings.

Headhunters are the top of the ladder, generally working in specific fields (mining, engineering, media, etc.) for companies seeking professional, even executive, employees at decidedly higher pay scales.

The higher up the food chain you go, the more the counselor is likely to know about the company, the job, and the interviewer.

Once an agency, recruiter, or headhunter believes you to be a qualified and serious candidate for a position (that is, you're going after a job for which you're qualified and, in her opinion, have a reasonable chance of getting hired), you can use them as great initial sources of information. In fact, questions that would be inappropriate or uncomfortable to ask on a "real" interview may be fine to ask a recruiter or headhunter.

Just remember that these counselors are working for the company—that's who's paying their fees and probably giving them dozens of medium- to high-level jobs to fill every year. So, ultimately, that's where their loyalties lie. Nevertheless, if they can supply a key client with its newest superstar—you—their stock will rise accordingly. (We won't mention what happens if you embarrass them on the job or, worse, on the interview, will we?)

Questions to ask agencies and recruiters

How long have you been working with this company?

The longer they've been on retainer, the more they know and the more they can tell you.

How many people have you placed there?

Is a written, detailed job description available?

Is this a new position? Was it created as part of a new project, division, or strategy?

New positions imply growth. Given the current economy, this would be surprising, but not unheard of. Any company growing now is one you want to work for!

If it's not a new posisiton, what happened to the person who held this job previously?

If they were fired, why? (And what can you learn from their failure?) If they were promoted, what did they do right? And where did they end up?

To whom would I be reporting? What can you tell me about him or her?

How many people would be reporting to me? What can you tell me about them?

What kind of a maelstrom are you diving into? It may be hard to get a truthful answer to this question from the headhunter, and harder still from the hiring manager, but don't walk blindly into a department that's heading for a meltdown.

How long has this job been open? How many candidates has the interviewer seen?

If the job has been open for months, and the interviewer has already seen dozens of candidates, no explanation is positive. Either the interviewer is fishing for someone who doesn't exist, can't make up his mind or keeps changing the description of what he's seeking. Or else the job, company, or staff is so scary candidates wind up running for the hills. Whichever the case, the longer the job has been open, the more suspicious you should be...and the more probing questions you should ask.

How long do you think the interview process for this job will take?

You know what I'm making and what I'd like to make. You know the kind of overall package I'm seeking. Do you foresee any problems with the company meeting my needs?

Would the recruiter send you on an interview with a company offering significantly less than he knows you require? Doubtful. But there's no reason for you to wait to ask this question until you've gone through a series of interviews at the company...only to discover that, *whoops!*, he did just that.

Is the person with whom I'm interviewing the decision-maker? If she isn't, who is?

Is the interviewer my potential boss?

If so, you won't necessarily approach the interview itself any differently, but you will certainly spend more time gauging the "chemistry" between the two of you.

What can you tell me about the culture of the company?

Before you set up an interview for me, could I meet with some of the other people you've already placed at this company?

Not all recruiters will welcome this question or respond positively to it. It delays their ability to get you in the door, a delay that may conceivably cost you the job (and him a commission). So, I would consider asking this question only if his answers to other questions have caused you to seriously doubt whether you want to interview there at all.

How integral to the success of the company is the department I'd be joining?

A positive answer is especially important to the more ambitious among you. If "your" department is the vital hub of the whole operation, it puts you in the middle of the action and greatly increases your chances to be seen, evaluated, appreciated, and promoted. On the other hand, a "support" department may be less pressured and less hectic...but less rewarding, too.

Is there anything else I need to know that would either doom my chances or help me ace the interview?

This is the last question you ask them. Give them one more chance to give you that magic elixir that will turn your interview experience into gold.

Why you should avoid Human Resources

There aren't many career books that will advise you to make a beeline for the Human Resources department of a company you've targeted. In fact, most, if not all, will tell you to avoid it like the plague if possible. What have these poor (formerly) personnel people done to generate such animosity?

Nothing, really. I'm sure many of them are very nice people, with loving families and pets, who do their jobs very well. The problem is that their jobs have little to do with actually getting *you* a job. They are *not* seeking candidates to interview and hire; they are trying to maximize the number they can *eliminate*. They are the screeners, the people who sift the sands of the known employment universe to discard the unqualified, the over-qualified, the under-qualified, and the misqualified. They can say no. And they do. A lot. But they *can't say* yes.

In addition to not being able to actually offer you anything more than coffee or tea (and maybe an IQ or drug test), many Human Resources departments may have (surprisingly) little idea about what hiring managers really want in job applicants. The more technical or specialized the field, the truer this statement.

I know of a Human Resources Director who recommended a candidate for whom English was a second—and not very *good*—language for the top editorial post on a major association magazine. Another passed along a candidate who got 55 out of 100 on a spelling test for a proofreading position. Still another recommended someone whose resume was filled with rather obvious or easily discovered lies for a Vice President of Finance position.

At many organizations, even hiring managers make it a point to go around their Human Resources departments—bringing candidates in, interviewing them, and only *then* passing them along so Human Resources can take care of the paperwork.

Make it easier for the hiring manager to do just that. Make every effort to get in touch with him or her directly, preferably by dropping the name of a "friend of a friend."

If you *have* to go through Human Resources (and sometimes despite your best efforts you will), you can't ignore their power: They're the only ones who can get you to the next level—the real interview. So it certainly would behoove you to make friends with them and use them in whatever way you can.

Staffers in the best departments can and do know more than they are sometimes given credit for. They know the company, they may know something about the job, they probably know whom you'll be working for, whom you'll be working with, whom you'll be supervising. They can steer you in the right direction and help you appreciate the culture you're about to confront.

The Personnel Manager at a major magazine publisher I worked for was such a veteran. She knew where all the bodies were buried...and who should join them. With her help and input, I became the first person without previous magazine experience ever hired at that company. I paid her back by not only becoming the youngest sales manager in the company's history, but doing it more quickly than anyone had ever done it.

Nevertheless, you will probably not go wrong if you presume that the Human Resources person conducting a screening interview has no time to become your best friend, knows little or nothing about the job you so desperately want, and knows even less about the hiring manager.

But it's worth asking many of the same questions you would ask a recruiter or employment agency, and a few others. (As always, these are *not* in any order):

What are your recruiting plans this year?
How is your recruiting going?

In other words, are they expanding? Do people want to work there? A talkative assistant might blithely confide in you that it's been difficult for them to find qualified candidates. Given the current nature of the economy and the growing ranks of the recently laid-off, that failure should give you pause: What do those candidates—the ones seemingly giving this company a wide berth—know that you don't?

What's a key thing about your company you'd like potential new hires to know?

What are the company's governing priorities? If the answer is a series of numbers—grosses, sales, profits, ratios—you've just discovered your place in the pecking order: the bottom line. Personally, I'd value (and survive) at a company that talked more about teamwork, the accomplishments of its people or its sense of social responsibility. Make sure the company values what *you* do, or it will be an unwieldy fit...and probably a short stay.

Tell me some of the particular skills or attributes that you want in the candidate for this position.

The answer should tell you how much the company values your traits. With this information, you can underline those traits you possess at the close of this interview—to end it on a strong note—and during the hiring interview.

Given my qualifications, skills and experience, do you have any concerns about my ability to become an important member of this company?

Probably not. If you didn't meet the summary of qualifications forwarded to Human Resources, you wouldn't be talking to anyone. But it never hurts to ask a question designed to uncover hidden objections. (See Chapter 6 for a much fuller discussion of this topic and a number of additional questions.)

How quickly are you hoping to fill this position?

Where are you in the decision-making process?

How would you say I stack up against the other candidates you've interviewed?

Can you tell me more about what I'd be doing on a daily basis?

How would you describe the corporate culture?

Can you tell me something about the interviewer?

Can you tell me something about my boss?

Can you tell me something about the people with whom I'll be working?

Can you tell me something about the people I'll be managing?

If you're going to be managing a significant number of people, it's unlikely you'd be forced to start in HR, but I've included this question here anyway.

Is this a new position? If it isn't: **What happened to the last person who held this job?**

Does the company have a mission statement or written philosophy? May I have a copy?

If not, consider the Chairman's message in the annual report the corporate mission statement.

Are there any challenges facing this department (your department, not HR) right now?

Do you have a written description of the position? I'd like to make sure I understand my duties, responsibilities, and the results you expect me to achieve.

This is a good question to pose to the screening interviewer (and a great way to ask it). It will help you prepare to face the hiring manager. If a written description doesn't exist, ask the interviewer to tell you what she considers the primary functions of the job.

Watch out for job descriptions that are too general, too elaborate, or too far-fetched. That doesn't mean you can't still be interested and interview, but it does mean you have to ask some clarifying questions. Why do companies lay out such god-awful descriptions? Why doesn't the hiring manager take the time to more clearly define the role he wants you to play (and then tell those poor people in Human Resources so *they* can do a better job of screening candidates)? It's a mystery.

What other positions at the company should this job prepare me for? Is that the career track my predecessors have followed?

You don't want to blindly condemn yourself to the fast track to nowhere. So find out how you can expect to advance after you land this job. What happened to the person you would be replacing? Is he or she still with the company? If so, doing what?

Try to pursue this line of questioning without giving the impression that you can't wait to get *out* of a job you don't even *have* yet! If you ask it in a completely non-threatening manner, your ambition will be understood, even welcomed.

At the end of this chapter I've included a more comprehensive list of questions to ask about the company, department, and position. Use it to craft your own list for Human Resources.

Am I overqualified?

This, of course, is a question you really should ask *yourself* before you go on *any* interview. It's essential to admit—at least to yourself—if you *are* seriously overqualified for a position. Many of you might think it's easier to get a job beneath your qualifications: to work as an accounting assistant when you've been a full-charge bookkeeper, to be a receptionist when you've been an office manager, to go back to sales after rising to sales manager.

It isn't. You may have more qualifications than the job requires, but you may no longer have the *specific* qualifications it *demands*. While you may have overseen a 20-person sales force and be known far and wide as an ace motivator, you will have trouble getting a job selling copy machines. Why? Because they don't *care* about your management and motivational credentials, nor do they need them. They want to know how many copy machines you're capable of selling a month. And they *do* care that you've never sold one!

Employers may question the motivation of someone willing to "do almost anything." Will such an employee just show up, do what's asked, and nothing more? What about someone willing to work "for almost nothing?" To quote another cliché: You get what you pay for. And that's exactly what "almost nothing" is worth.

Especially in lower-level jobs, employers want people who are happy to be doing what they were hired to do, not constantly looking around and commenting how they could do the boss's job better than he could. The office manager wants to treat the receptionist as a receptionist, not someone who has been an office manager and may, indeed, know more than he does about running an office. Just as some managers worry about hiring underlings who they fear may one day outshine them, many people worry about hiring people for low-level jobs who have already done what their boss is doing. It's disconcerting and, to many, highly threatening.

You may be screened by phone or in person

Whether you are preparing for a "pre-interview" with an employment agency, recruiter, headhunter, or Human Resources, your initial interview may be on the phone or in person.

Telephone screening is an effective tactic used by many interviewers. Some interviewers, however, rely on the strategy as a *primary* means of qualifying candidates. For many of these interviewers, the in-person interview is little more than an opportunity to confirm what they feel they've already learned on the phone.

Interviewers who typically fall into this category are entrepreneurs, CEOs, high-level executives, and others short on time and long on vision. Their guiding philosophy could be summed up as: "My time is at a premium, I have a personnel problem to solve, and I don't plan to waste my valuable time talking in person to anybody but the very best."

A telephone screener is also often the dominant interviewer at small- to mid-sized companies where no formal Human Resources (or Personnel) department exists or where such a department has only recently been created. The primary objective of the telephone screener is to *identify reasons to remove you from active consideration* before *scheduling an in-person meeting.*

Common reasons for abrupt removal from the telephone screener's short list include:

❑ Evidence that there's a disparity between your resume and actual experience.

❑ Poor verbal communication skills.

❑ Lack of required technical skills.

Conversations with the oh-so-busy telephone screener are often quite abrupt. These people tend to have a lot on their plates. But you don't mind, do you? What could be better than answering questions from the comfort of your own home?

For starters, conducting a telephone interview has cost you two valuable tools you have to work with during in-person interviews: eye contact and body language. You're left with your skills, the facts on your resume, and your ability to communicate verbally.

Don't be discouraged. *Always* project a positive image through your voice and your answers. Don't overdo it, but don't let the telephone be your undoing either. If your confidence is flagging, try smiling while you listen and speak. Sure, it might look silly—but it works, and the screener can't see you anyway!

Another important point: You have a right to be prepared for any interview. Chances are, the interviewer will call you to set a time for the telephone interview. However, if she wants to plow right into it as soon as you answer the phone, there's nothing wrong with asking if she could call back at a mutually agreeable time. You need to prepare your surroundings for a successful interview. If the kids are fighting in the background, you're expecting a package, or call waiting keeps beeping and interrupting, you'll be flustered before you start. So don't start. Have the interviewer call you back.

Did the interviewer dial a wrong number?

The main rule most telephone screeners follow (or are taught to follow) is *not* to extend an offer for a face-to-face interview to anyone they feel is not well-suited for the position or the company. If the phone interview has led them to this conclusion, there are two ways they will try to wrap up. The first is to let you down easy:

> *"Mike, I really appreciate your taking the time to talk about your background with me today. You've given me plenty to think about. You should know, though, that this is a very competitive position, and that we'll be talking to a lot of people over the next week or so.*
>
> *"I think the way I'd like to leave this is that if we feel there's the possibility of a*

> *good match for this position or for any other*
> *opening, we can get back in touch with you*
> *at this number. Does that make sense?"*

There is another school of thought about the best way to conclude a screening conversation—the direct approach (which I personally favor). It could go something like this:

> *"Mike, I've listened carefully to what you've*
> *told me today, and I have to be honest with*
> *you—I don't think we have a good match*
> *here. We're going to have to take a pass this*
> *time around."*

What can you do to fight off either of these brush-offs?

In the first instance, the door has been left at least a little ajar. So a truly aggressive rejoinder is not called for. Nevertheless, you cannot allow the screener to hang up without finding some way to actually get *in* that door—to make him reconsider. Here's one way to accomplish that:

> *"Mr. Billingsly, I appreciate how hectic your*
> *schedule is, but I think we would both benefit if*
> *you could spare me some time to meet in per-*
> *son. May I call your secretary to schedule a brief*
> *15-minute meeting for next week with you?"*

If the interviewer is a soft touch at heart, the very fact that you resisted his attempt to brush you off might make him relent. Even a tougher interviewer, though, would be impressed with the confident tone you struck ("we would both benefit"), the understanding you demonstrated ("hectic schedule") and the modest request you made ("15 minutes").

In the second instance, you have to be more aggressive because the interviewer is being more aggressive. Try something like this:

> *"Mr. Herman, I'm surprised to hear you say that. I must have done a poor job communicating the credentials that make me perfect for this job and my enthusiasm for it.*
>
> *"We obviously need to meet in person to discuss this more. Which would be better for you, Monday at 10 or Tuesday at 3?"*

Did it ever occur to you that Herman's aggressive brush-off could be a conscious strategy, an attempt to gauge how you will respond to such outright rejection? If you're applying for a sales position, I wouldn't be at all surprised if it were. And if you just rolled over and accepted his brush off, then the interviewer would conclude you *couldn't* handle rejection (a huge factor in sales) and *wouldn't* be right for the job after all. Respond to an aggressive brush-off by being equally aggressive. The alternative is unappetizing—just to hang up and move on to the next interview.

Many Human Resources and Personnel professionals fall into a different category: human screens. For them, interviewing is not simply a once-a-quarter or once-a-month event, but rather a key part of their daily job descriptions. They meet and interview many people, and are more likely than a telephone screener to consider an exceptional applicant for more than one opening within the organization.

A primary objective of a human screen is to *develop a strong group of candidates for managers* (the third kind of interviewer) *to interview in person.* To do this, of course, they must fend off many applicants and callers—a daunting task, because the human screen or the department in which he works is often the only contact provided in employment advertisements.

Among the most common reasons for removal from a human screen's "hot" list:

❐ Lack of the formal or informal qualifications outlined in the organization's job description.

❐ Sudden changes in hiring priorities and/or personnel requirements.

❐ Poor performance during the in-person interview.

❐ Inaction due to uncertainty about your current status or contact information.

That last reason is more common than you might imagine. Human screens are constantly swamped with phone calls, resumes, and unannounced visits from hopeful applicants. Odds are that despite their best efforts, they sometimes lose track of qualified people.

Human screens excel at separating the wheat from the chaff. Because they are exposed to a wide variety of candidates on a regular basis, they usually boast more face-to-face interviewing experience than members of the other two groups. They may be more likely to spot inconsistencies or outright lies on resumes, simply because they've seen so many over the years that they know when a candidate's credentials for a given position don't quite pass the "smell test."

And although interviews with a telephone screener or the hiring manager may be rushed because of their hectic schedules, human screens are often able to spend a comparatively long amount of time with particularly qualified candidates.

However, these interviewers often do not have direct knowledge of the day-to-day requirements of the job to be filled. They have formal summaries, of course, but they often don't possess the same first-hand familiarity with the skills, temperament, and outlook necessary for success on the job. Typically one step away from the action, they're generally reliant on job postings and experience summaries.

If those formal outlines are imperfectly written, and if human screens receive no direct input from supervisors on the kinds of people they're seeking, you may be passed through the process even though you're not particularly qualified (or eliminated even though you are).

Not surprisingly, human screens often react with a puzzled look if others ask them to offer their "gut reaction" about a particular candidate. Because they're generally operating removed from the work itself, they often prefer quantifying their assessments of candidates in hard numbers: either the candidate *does* have three years of appropriate experience, or she *doesn't.* Either she *has* been trained in computer design, or she *hasn't.* Of course, this analysis may overlook important interpersonal issues.

Don't believe everything you read

And don't believe everything company representatives tell you. Just as employees have been known to "forget" a job when writing their resume and slightly exaggerate their responsibilities, employers have been known to tell attractive candidates what *they* want to hear.

"Need your space and independence? Like to work in a freewheeling, open kind of atmosphere. Hey, that's us!" Except, unfortunately, for the one Neanderthal who just happens to be...your prospective boss.

It happened to my wife. Though at one time we both wound up working for the same magazine publishing company, we experienced totally different corporate cultures.

One reason was because I was in corporate head-quarters (New York) and she was based in an outpost (Chicago). I had 400 people around me, including all the major executives and the two owners. She had seven other salespeople and a secretary around her. Whatever answers she got about the "corporate culture" would have born little resemblance to the reality she lived.

She also had one of the previous "Neanderthal" bosses who, again, bore no resemblance to anyone else I ever worked with or for at that company. As a result, while I was in an environment that allowed me freedom and the ability to pretty much set my own priorities and schedule, she was virtually a prisoner of the time sheet and subject to frequent bullying rants.

Companies sometimes consciously misstate job requirements in their advertisements so as to attract, they believe, the "higher end" of the applicant pool.

If their gut feeling is that the job requires two years of experience, they may say three are required, expecting a higher grade of queries and assuming that the few people who do contact them with only two years of experience are likely to be more motivated than the average applicant.

This is called an "enhanced excluder," a means of setting the bar *slightly* higher than they need to, knowing they can always ignore the standards they've set for the right candidate. Some companies use this method almost as a pre-interviewing technique, a way to see which applicants try to get around the announced requirements...and how compelling a case they can make for themselves.

If candidates absolutely, positively, *have* to have very particular technical expertise, that requirement should be prominently and specifically featured in the advertisement. This sounds self-evident, but you'd be surprised at the number of hiring managers I've spoken to who *don't* specify particular skills they're seeking...and then complain about the experience levels of the candidates they interview. Ambiguous statements such as "good computer skills" don't help an employer attract the skilled people it's seeking. And they certainly don't help *you* figure out whether you're qualified for the position!

An organized list of questions

Here is a comprehensive list of questions to ask about the company, department, and/or job. Some may have already been answered through your research, some may be pertinent for the Human Resources screener, some may be more pertinent for the hiring manager. In any case, add them to your list of smart questions!

> ### Questions about the company

What are your leading products or services?

What products or services are you planning to introduce in the near future?

What are your key markets? Are they growing?

Will you be entering any new markets in the next couple of years? Which ones and via what types of distribution channels?

What growth rate are you anticipating? Will this be accomplished internally or through acquisitions?

How many employees work for the organization? In how many offices? In this office?

Are you planning any acquisitions?

What has been your layoff history in the last five years? Do you anticipate any cutbacks in the near future and, if you do, how will they impact my department or position?

What major problems or challenges have you recently faced? How were they addressed? What results do you expect?

What is your share of each of your markets?

Which other companies serving those markets pose a serious threat?

What is your hiring philosophy?

What are your plans and prospects for growth and expansion?

What are your goals in the next few years?

What do *you* like best about this company? Why?

What is your ranking within the industry? Does this represent a change from where it was a year or a few years ago?

Questions about the department

Could you explain the organizational structure of the department and its primary functions and responsibilities?

To whom will I be reporting? To whom does he or she report?

With which other departments would I work most closely?

How many people work exclusively in this department?

What problems is this department facing? What are its current goals and objectives?

Questions about the job

What kind of training should I expect and for how long?

Do you offer reimbursement for job-related education? Time off?

How many people will be reporting to me?

Is relocation an option, a possibility, or a requirement?

How did this job become available? Was the previous person promoted? What is their new title? Was the previous person fired? Why?

Would I be able to speak with the person who held this job previously?

Could you describe a typical day in this position?

How long has this position been available?

Is there no one from within the organization who is qualified for this position?

Where will I be working? May I see my office/cubicle?

How advanced/current is the hardware and software I will be expected to use?

How much day-to-day autonomy will I have?

Does this job usually lead to other positions in the company? Which ones?

Please tell me a little bit about the people with whom I'll be working most closely.

Questions about the next step

How many other candidates have you interviewed? How many more will you be interviewing before you expect to make a decision?

Before you're able to reach a hiring decision, how many more interviews should I expect to go through and with whom?

With whom will I be meeting next (names and job titles)?

What issues are important to each of them?

What are they like?

Are they amiable, laid back, hard-charging? You want to be ready for the personality you're going to face. Won't you act differently with a fire-breathing sales type than you would with a mild-mannered bean counter? Of course you would. Additionally, you won't want to overemphasize your computer expertise with the guy who's computer illiterate—it'll just make him feel inferior...to a potential inferior.

What are their ages and family situations?

You would not ask this question of a hiring manager or anyone else with direct input into the hiring decision. Because *they* can't, by law, ask you these types of questions, you would (I hope) be careful to avoid such personal questions yourself. But even though it's a small risk, I think it's worth it to get whatever such information you can from the "lower-level" interviewers. The more you know, the more you can prepare.

How long have they been with the company?

If the interviewer is middle-aged and in a middle management position at a smaller company, he's either not the most ambitious person you ever met or has "risen to the level of his incompetence." You may want to make him feel secure—not come on too strong—because he's probably aware he isn't moving any higher.

On the other hand, if you're interviewing with a 27-year-old vice president who clearly seems destined for better things (and higher levels), you'll want to convince her that you're someone she'll want to bring along for the ride, someone who can perhaps make her own rise quicker or easier because of the talents you can add to her team.

You may not be able to find out the answers to all or even most of these personal questions, but you will certainly get helpful answers to some if you only ask whomever arranged the interview. *Whatever* they tell you will be more than you knew before!

Based on the answers you receive to these kinds of questions, try to create a "model" of the person with whom you'll be meeting—what she looks like, what makes her smile, what makes her angry, how she deals with stress, what seems important to her, what she'd laugh off.

Using this admittedly hypothetical "pseudo-interviewer," picture yourself actually in the interview with her. Answer her questions. Ask yours. Counter her objections. Ask for the job! Even if the eventual reality bares little or no resemblance to the model you've constructed, doing this exercise has to make you better prepared than just walking in cold.

All the research, assessment, and preparation is over. It's time for the real thing: your interview with the hiring manager.

Questions TO ASK
Your NEW BOSS

The hiring manager may not be the person for whom you will be working, but probably will be. Even where others have strong input, most companies still allow managers to hire their own staff, within certain parameters. He is probably a supervisor who has chosen (or is required) to shoehorn in-person interviews into his busy workdays. In smaller companies especially, the president may be the ultimate decision maker, even if you won't be reporting to her.

What's different about interviewing with the hiring manager as opposed to your time with a recruiter or headhunter or even Human Resources? This is the person you actually have to impress, the only one who can say those magic words, "You're hired. When can you start?" This is the person you have to be careful with.

The hiring manager's primary objective is to *evaluate your skills and measure your personal chemistry on a first-hand basis.* These interviewers want to get to know everything they can about the people with whom they'll be closely working. (As we've seen, the telephone screener, by contrast, may well be an entrepreneur who delegates heavily and interacts only intermittently with new hires. And the human screen has nothing to do with the day-to-day operation of the company.)

Common reasons for being dropped from a hiring manager's "hot" list include:

❑ Lack of personal chemistry or rapport;

❑ Poor performance during the interview itself;

❑ Her assessment that you, although qualified and personable, would simply not fit in well with the team.

Many hiring managers have an excellent intuitive sense of who will (and won't) be likely to perform the job well and achieve a good "fit" with the rest of the work group. On the other hand, it sometimes comes as a surprise to applicants that excellent supervisors can be less than stellar interviewers, but a great many managers lack any formal training in the art of interviewing.

Of the three categories of interviewers, this is the group most likely to interpret the interview as an opportunity to "get to know" more about you—rather than to require specific answers to questions about your background, experience, outlook on work, and interpersonal skills.

The hiring interview

Your first interview with the person who will manage your prospective position is not likely to be a walk in the park. You may be stepping out of the range of the experience and interviewing talent of the Human Resources professional—into unknown territory.

And you could wander there for a while...

Why? Experienced interviewers are trained to stay in charge of the interview, not let it meander down some dead-end, nonproductive track. There is a predictability to the way they conduct interviews, even if they wield different techniques.

On the other hand, the hiring manager is sure to lack some or all of the screening interviewer's knowledge, experience, and skill—making him an unpredictable animal.

The vast majority of corporate managers don't know what it takes to hire the right candidate. Few of them have had formal training in conducting interviews of any kind. To make things worse, most managers feel slightly less comfortable conducting the interview than the nervous candidate sitting across their desks from them!

For example, a manager might decide you are not the right person for the job, without ever realizing that the questions he or she asked were so ambiguous, or so off the mark, that even the perfect candidate could not have returned the "right" answers. No one monitors the performance of the interviewer. And the candidate cannot be a mind reader. So more often than is necessary, otherwise perfectly qualified candidates walk out the door for good simply because the manager failed at the interview!

Foiling the inept interviewer

But that doesn't have to happen to you. You can—and should—be prepared to put your best foot forward, despite the inexperience of the manager interviewing you. That begins with having ready answers to the 101 questions he's likely to ask. But it doesn't stop there. The interviewer may not ask *any* of these questions.

You'll be a step ahead of the game (and the other candidates) if you realize at the outset that the interviewer is after more than just facts about your skills and background. He is waiting for something more elusive to hit him, something he may not even be able to articulate. He wants to feel that somehow, you "fit" the organization or department.

Talk about a tough hurdle! But knowing what you're up against is half the battle. Rather than sit back passively and hope for the best, you can help the unskilled interviewer focus on how your unique skills can directly benefit—"fit"— the department or organization using a number of specific examples. And a number of smart questions.

What the interviewer wants to see and hear

What will the hiring manager be looking and listening for, right from the moment she meets you? Here's the advice *I* gave her in my book, *Ask the Right Questions, Hire the Best People*:

What to look for: the initial greeting

When you first encounter the candidate, silently ask yourself questions like the ones in the following list. The more often you can answer "yes," the more likely it is that you've hooked up with a poised, confident candidate. Of course, no one is suggesting that confidence and social grace can compensate for a lack of ability in the workplace. But, in a perfect world, wouldn't you prefer to work with someone who meets all the formal qualifications...*and* has enough self-confidence to interact effectively with others?

❖ Did the candidate grip your hand firmly, avoiding both the "bone-crusher" and the "wet fish" approach?

❖ Did the candidate shake your hand with a sense of purpose?

❖ Did the candidate hold the shake for an appropriate period—neither too short nor too long? (Three shakes is sufficient.)

❖ Did the candidate use one hand? (A two-handed shake is usually regarded as a sign of over-familiarity at the outset of the first meeting, though there are some regional/ cultural exceptions to this rule.)

❖ Did the candidate look you in the eye?

❖ Did the candidate smile?

❖ Did the candidate use your name when greeting you?

What to look for: body language

Once the candidate takes a seat, you'll be doing the lion's share of the talking to begin the meeting. *After* you have put the person at ease by asking a few rapport-building questions, begin to monitor his or her gaze, physical posture and general bearing. Use the questions below as a rough guideline, and make discreet notes as the interview moves forward. The more "yes" answers you record, the more comfortable (and, presumably, forthcoming) the person is likely to feel interacting with you.

❖ Does the candidate make appropriate intermittent eye contact with you—neither staring you down nor avoiding your gaze?

❖ Is eye contact broken only at natural points in the discussion, rather than suddenly, in the middle of an exchange?

❖ Is the candidate's mouth relaxed? (A tightly clenched jaw, pursed lips or a forced, unnatural smile may indicate problems handling stress.)

❖ Is the candidate's forehead and eyebrow area relaxed? (Ditto.)

❖ Does the candidate occasionally smile naturally?

❖ Does the person avoid nodding very rapidly for long periods of time while you're speaking? (This is shorthand for "Be quiet and let me say something now," and it is inappropriate in an interview setting.)

❖ Does the candidate move his or her hands so much or in such a weird manner that you actually notice? (Constant twitching of the fingers-or even worse, knuckle-cracking-may mean you're dealing with a person who simply can't calm down. Yes, an interview is an unsettling experience, but so are some of the tasks this person will have to perform on the job!)

❖ On a similar note, does the candidate avoid shuffling and tapping his or her feet?

❖ Is the candidate's posture good? (Chair-slumpers send an unfortunate silent message: "I'm not even trying to make a good impression." If you hire them, you may encounter that message on a daily basis.)

❖ Are the candidate's eyes usually gazing forward, rather than darting all over the room?

❖ Is the candidate's head upright?

❖ Does the candidate tend to sit with crossed arms? (This may signal either a confrontational attitude or a sense of deep insecurity, neither of which is a great sign.)

❖ Does the person appear to be breathing regularly and deeply?

❖ Is the person's personal hygiene and grooming acceptable? (In other words, would you want to sit next to this person during a long meeting? Ask yourself: If the candidate won't make an effort to clean up his or her act for a job interview, what will the average workday be like?)

What to listen for

What the candidate says is certainly important, but so is *how* he or she says it. Make circumspect written notes if you cannot answer "yes" to all of the following questions during the interview. Three or more such notes during the course of a half-hour interview could indicate a problem with social skills.

❖ Does the candidate respond in a clear, comprehensible, and confident tone of voice?

❖ Does the candidate avoid prolonged pauses in the middle of sentences?

❖ Is the candidate's speaking rhythm consistent and appropriate?

❖ Does the candidate avoid rambling answers?

❖ Does each of the candidate's answers have a clear concluding point or do they all seem to just trail off into nothingness?

❖ Does the candidate avoid interrupting you? (Breaking in while a representative of a prospective future employer is speaking shows poor judgment and underdeveloped people skills.)

❖ Does the candidate take time to consider difficult questions before plunging in to answer them?

❖ Does the candidate ask for additional information or clarification when dealing with complex or incomplete questions?

❖ Does the candidate offer answers that are consistent with one another?

As you monitor nonverbal signals during the interview, bear in mind that physical actions and vocal delivery should support the answers the interviewee passes along. A candidate who assures you that he has what it takes to ride the ups and downs of a career in sales, but looks pale and shellshocked when you mention that you're interviewing other candidates, is sending two very different messages. The "lyrics" may be saying "I can handle rejection," but the "music" doesn't quite support that contention!

If that's what the interviewer is looking and listening for, you'd better be aware of the signals you're sending!

Smart interview questions for your new boss

Basic questions

Revisit those basic questions you tried to answer through your research and those you asked about the company and department of the agency, recruiter, headhunter or Human Resources department. If you've gotten satisfactory answers to them, you don't need to ask them again.

Whatever questions remain from this first list, ask. Then add a few more:

> **Please explain the (department, division) company's organizational chart.**
>
> **Can you give me a more detailed understanding of what my days might be like?**
>
> **What are the department's specific objectives for the next three months (the length of your probable probation period)?**

After you hear them, of course, you will do two things: Wrack your brain for specific examples from your experience or education that will convince him *you* can help him *reach* those goals. And ask more follow-up questions about how your job responsibilities will impact them.

You and (one of his important competitors) have many similar products (or offer similar services). What sets you apart from them? What's different about the way you do things? What's different about their corporate structure, missionor philosophy?

How fast is the company growing? Is management happy with that rate, or do you have expansion plans in mind?

Growth can be a double-edged sword: Faster top-line growth (that is, greater sales) could mean greater opportunity to climb the career ladder faster than usual. It could also characterize a company that spends itself into oblivion trying to buy sales. (See "dot.com.")

What is the company's ranking within the industry? Does this position represent a change from where it was a few years ago?

You should already have some indication of the answer to this question from your initial research, particularly if the company is publicly owned. If you have some of this information, go ahead and build it into your question: *"I've read that the company has risen from fifth to second in market share in just the past three years. What are the key reasons for this dramatic success?"*

How do you see me working with each of the department heads?

How would my performance be measured in this position? How is the department's performance measured?

Probing questions

The previous basic questions, and many of those you asked during your research or while interviewing with an agency, recruiter, headhunter or screening interviewer, are almost solely to fill in your overall portrait of the company as a whole. Once you have established in your own mind that you are truly interested in the company, you'll want to ask detailed questions designed to elicit specific information about the department, the job and the people:

What are the things you would most like to see changed in this (section, department, group, division, company)?

When may I meet some of my potential colleagues (or subordinates)? Are they part of the interviewing process here?

Given the economic environment as I write this, it is likely the answer to the latter question is yes because the manager certainly doesn't want to hire a loser when there are so many winners being laid off every day (through little or no fault of their own). But there *are* companies where the answer would be "yes" under almost *any* circumstances. Those are the ones I like. Why? Because including "lower-level" employees in the process proves that the company values its employees' opinion and realizes that just adding some stranger to the team by executive fiat isn't an effective way to show your employees how important they are to you. Nor does it do much for "team building" or any of those other corporate mantras that get thrown around.

How will you weigh your subordinates' input with your own assessment of my candidacy?

Or (to the subordinates):

What kind of feedback does your boss expect you to give him? How much weight has he given it in the past?

You can never be sure how much influence anyone has with the ultimate decision-maker. I once interviewed at a company where a prospective new salesperson had to meet briefly with each of the seven sales managers, although the Vice President of Sales was the ultimate decision maker. Well, one of the two female managers—not the best or the brightest, I might add—was sleeping with the boss. I'm not sure how I would have ever found that out (it took me a few months at the company before the gossip reached my virginal ears), but it tends to emphasize the importance of treating everyone you meet with courtesy, respect, and professionalism. And realizing that you can't easily discern who is going to be a key factor in your hiring...or your being passed over.

Even if the lady weren't sleeping with the boss, I guarantee if three or maybe even two of the sales managers had decided I "wouldn't fit in," that particular VP would have never hired me. Some bosses are more influenced than others. Which leads to a good question if you're put in a similar situation:

Are there many after-hours business events I will be expected to attend?

How much travel should I expect to do in a typical month? Are there distinct periods of heavier travel?

Do you have a lot of employees working flextime or telecommuting?

Make sure you're careful not to imply this is one of your requirements, especially if the answer is a frosty, "No. 9 to 6, and I value punctuality."

What has the turnover been in this department in the last couple of years?

Warning, Will Robinson! You're about to join a department that goes through salespeople like water through a hose. Who cares about the size of your raise and bonus if you won't be there in 60 days?

How many hours a week do you expect your star employees to put in? How much overtime does this position typically involve? How many weekends a year would I be expected to work?

Please tell me about the people with whom I'll be working most closely.

I wish someone had told me about this question before my last job interview! The answer can tell you so many things: How good your potential colleagues really are at their jobs, how much you are likely to learn from them and, most important, whether the hiring manager seems enthusiastic about his team.

A hiring manager usually tries to put on his best face during an interview, just like you. But catching the interviewer off guard with this question may give you a glimpse of the real feelings hiding behind her "game face."

If he doesn't seem very enthusiastic about his current team, it may not be one you'll be particularly thrilled to join. This hiring manager may attribute little success, and perhaps a lot of headaches, to the people who work for her. Is that the kind of boss you want?

How much budgetary responsibility would I have?

I don't care if you're interviewing for the lowest position in the organization and the answer is, "Are you kidding? You can't buy paper clips without submitting a six-part form and getting 14 signatures!" The question shows that you are willing to take responsibility and understand the importance of doing so in order to move up the career ladder. Ask it.

Can you give me a better idea of the kinds of decisions I could make (or amounts of money I could spend) without oversight?

This is a question for anyone *above* the lowest level—it will help clarify what level of "power" you're *really* being handed and give you greater insight into how centralized the company is. If you are at a fairly high level (manager, director, VP) and the answer is, "Oh, anything under $100. After that, you have to check with me," you may have just learned more than you really wanted to know about the limitations of your "power." In fact, at that supposed level, such an answer should send you running for the hills. I know *receptionists* who have more discretionary power!

Similarly, if you expect to have people reporting to you, your ability to hire and fire, and your involvement in interviewing candidates for your own team should reflect your level of management but will also reflect the corporate structure and culture.

I once worked for a medium-sized trade magazine publisher (400 people at headquarters, 100 more in regional offices) at which only the two owners had private secretaries. Everyone else, including the Vice Presidents of Sales, Operations, Production, Circulation, and Editorial shared secretaries. Even after I reached management level, I was still sharing a secretary with one other manager and three salespeople!

What would you like to be able to say about your new hire one year from now?

How has this job been performed in the past?

What do you see as the key challenges facing the company? My department?

How do you see my role evolving in the first two years? What would be the most logical areas for me to evolve into?

What do you think my biggest challenge will be if I start working for you?

Now, if a manager takes this question personally, interpreting it as "What problems am I going to have with *you*?" that would tell me something about the manager. Perhaps he's a little self-centered? Perhaps he's prone to define *your* "success" by how well you get along with *him*, as opposed to how well you do your job?

On the other hand, she may blurt out, "Roberta" or some other name you soon find out is the "problem" member of the team. *Your* potential team.

Or it may just elicit a detailed monologue about competition, products, services, the economy.

Whatever answer you get should give you a much better idea of how this interviewer thinks as a boss and what he sees as the focus of *his* job.

It's a matter of style

Even if you are comfortable with the job, the department, and the company—and have had most or all of your questions about them answered—never underestimate the importance of your boss's "style," the corporate culture, and how you will mesh with both. The next two sections offer questions to make sure you wind up with a comfy fit:

How would you describe your management style? Would you say that it's similar to others

in the organization, or do you consider yourself a bit of a maverick?

When's the last time you got really angry at one of your subordinates? What was the cause? What did you do? Has anything similar happened since? Did you react differently?

In your experience, are there particular types of people you seem to work better with than others?

This is a not-so-veiled attempt to "define" yourself according to the attributes the manager cites, presuming, of course, that the "type" of person he describes isn't so removed from your own personality as to be laughable.

What particular traits do you value most in your subordinates?

Again, tell me what you want to hear, Mr. Manager, so I can tell you that I'm all that!

What kinds of people seem to succeed in this company? In this department? Working for you?

How do you define success?

Tell me about the last time one of your subordinates made a major mistake. What did he or she do? What did you do? How did

that work out? What's your philosophy about "mistakes?"

How do you measure your own success?

What do you think your responsibility is to develop your people? Would you cite some examples of which you're particularly proud?

Questions about the culture, chemistry, fit

What have you enjoyed most about working here? What have you liked least? What do *you* like best about this company? Why?

If the interviewer hems and haws a lot over these questions, it may indicate that she doesn't really like the company that much at all.

If she's instantly enthusiastic, her answer should help sell you on her and the company.

The answer to these questions can also give you a good sense of the values of the organization and the hiring manager. If she talks about nothing but products and how well her stock options are doing, it may indicate a lack of enthusiasm for the "people side" of the business.

What is your history with the company?

What's keeping you here now?

There are plenty of reasons to ask this question and to ask it early. You'll get a better feel for where the interviewer came from—up through the ranks (and what specific rungs along the way) or from outside, for example. How long has he stayed at each position? Is he a mover and shaker or a plodder? Has she been at the company long enough to give you an accurate feel of its culture?

The second question is an especially important one to ask of the person to whom you'll be reporting. Again, if the word "people" isn't part of her answer, what does that tell you about her leadership or management style? If the reasons are all financial, I would question her dedication to the core culture...and even whether I could count on her sticking around if someone dangled a bigger carrot in her face.

Semi-closing questions

In the next chapter, we'll discuss in far more detail how to identify hidden objections to your candidacy, how to confront them, and how to ask for the job offer—questions designed to "close the sale." But there are questions a step below (or before, if you prefer), what I've called "semi-closing questions," that are designed to indicate your strong interest in the position and elicit more of the information you need to weigh a potential offer:

Are there problems that keep you awake?

Follow up: What could I do to make you sleep better? Alternate: How could I help you do a better job?

How will we work together to establish objectives and deadlines in the first months of this job?

This is a nice way to find out how much input you will have or whether you're heading into a fait accompli—"Glad you're here, Ron. Here's the plan for the next three months. Do it."

Do my qualifications, experience, education, demeanor, outlook, etc. remind you of another employee who succeeded at this job?

What are your own goals for the coming year? How do you think I could specifically help you achieve them?

If you were I, what are the three specific goals you would set for your first three months on the job?

What are three things that need immediate attention?

What skills are in short supply here?

Are there other things you would like someone to do that are not considered "formal" parts of the job?

What is the first problem I should tackle?

What's the one thing I can do right at this job to assure my success? What's the one thing that would assure failure?

Would it be possible to talk with _____ (the other department heads with whom I'd be working, my team, my boss, some of my potential colleagues/peers)?

Isn't there anything else you feel it is vital I know about the company (department, job, your expectations, etc.)?

This is the last "non-closing" question to ask. It is designed to give the interviewer every opportunity to tell you anything else he deems important.

A little knowledge *is* powerful

The more research you've done, the easier it will be to incorporate what you know into great questions. In the same vein, the way you phrase a question can effectively show the interviewer how well you've been listening and absorbing his pearls of wisdom:

> *"The job seems to be in a state of flux. What's your impression?"*

> *"Although your ad indicated that computer experience was the primary qualification, I get the impression from our talk so far that building a new team is your major concern. Do you agree?"*

"Your company appears to be (team-oriented, helter skelter, highly charged, serious, fun, etc.). Do you think that's an accurate assessment? If yes, can you tell me more about how that culture will impact how I work? If no, how would you describe it?"

Timing can be everything

If the absolutely perfect candidate walked in the door the day after a new position opened up, I don't know any hiring managers who would simply hire him on the spot and tell everyone else to pound salt. Even if he was everything the manager could have ever asked for...and more! Why? Human nature: "I've got to see more than one candidate or I won't have anyone to compare him to. How can I just hire the first person who comes through the door? What would my boss think? That I'm too impulsive? Giving the interviewing process short shrift? A poor interviewer?"

Better to be near the end of the process, so your enthusiasm and passion are fresh in the interviewer's mind, than to be a long-forgotten "perfect" candidate.

The further along they are in the process, the better it probably is for you. Ever watch an ice skating competition? No one wants to go first, do they? (And the champ never does, does she? *Hmmm.*) Why? Even if the first skater was flawless, crafting a performance that screamed for straight 6.0s, she'll never get them. If the judges gave *her* the highest marks, what would they do if one of the skaters who followed did an even *better* performance?

Chapter 6

Questions TO Close THE SALE

At some point, it will dawn on you that you actually *want* this job. You may even have gotten the impression that the *interviewer* wants you to have the job. Or at least you think she does.

It's time to find out how real your chances are by asking "closing" questions—highly targeted questions designed to uncover the interviewer's (unstated) concerns, figure out where you are in the process, identify the competition and, most important, ask for the job!

"Is there anyone else...?"

Salespeople know that one of the most important obstacles to "closing" a sale is talking to the wrong person. What good is a powerful, professional presentation that generates a series of enthusiastic "yes's" if the person you're selling lacks the authority to actually buy your product or service? While it may be important to get this person's recommendation, wouldn't *you* want to know you're actually interviewing with the person with the ability to say, "Great! When can you start?"

To forestall this waste of time and effort, top sales-people will often use a line like the following to qualify their prospect *before* they go into their spiel: *"Is there anyone else along with yourself who needs to be part of this discussion so a decision can be made today?"*

That's qualifying! Be ready to ask a similar question yourself:

Is there anyone else along with yourself
who needs to be part of this interview so
a *hiring* decision can be made today?

If the answer is no, you can feel somewhat confident that this is the person you have to convince. Often, an employer will answer a question such as this by detailing the hiring process for you:

> *"Well, Jim, I'm ultimately going to be the one making the decision about whom to hire, but I'm going to have the top two or three candidates interview with _____ and _____ before I make the final cut."*

Which would, of course, lead to a whole series of other questions:

> *"Will those other interviews be scheduled following this one?"*
>
> *"Over what period of time will those other interviews take place?"*
>
> *"How long a period have you set aside for interviews before you make a final decision?*
>
> *At what point do you feel you will be making a final decision?"*

"May I make appointments with those other ex-ecutives immediately following this interview?"

If you properly researched the interviewer and asked the right questions of the recruiter or headhunter with whom you're working (or the Human Resources person who pre-interviewed you), you really should already know whether the person you're talking to is the ultimate decision-maker. In an ideal world, of course. But the world these days is far from ideal and, in this economy, even the final decision-makers are hedging their bets. So ask this qualifying question early in the interview—it's important to know whether you're selling the Emperor...or merely one of the advisors to the throne.

Uncover hidden objections

Salespeople also know (or quickly learn) that the key to any sale is filling their customers' needs...or at least convincing the customer that they *can* fulfill those needs. In order to get to that point, however, they may have to handle a series of objections. In order to *answer* these objections, they must be *known*. Needless to say, not every buyer is blithely ready to volunteer the real reasons why he's unwilling to switch vendors (or the "magic" words that will win his business).

So, successful salespeople have developed detailed routines to elicit *hidden objections*—the unstated but real obstacles they must overcome to win the account. You must follow their lead. After all, you can't overcome an objection you don't even know about.

Questions designed to clear your path are, by their very nature, a little intrusive, a little pushy, a little aggressive. But they must be asked:

Is there anything that is stopping you from offering me this job right now?

Perhaps one of the more aggressive ways to phrase this question, but it certainly gets to the point. The interviewer may not bare his soul; he could answer, *"Yes, because you have three more interviews to go if you get past me!"* But at least you'll learn that much!

How do I compare with the others you've interviewed for this position?

or

How many other people would you say are also serious candidates for this position? How do you see me stacking up against them?

You can't really "knock" the competition, even if you wanted to (and you shouldn't want to), because no matter how much he tells you, you really won't know enough to do so. But it's essential that you know how many viable candidates there actually are and how the interviewer thinks you measure up. Invariably, rather than giving you a plethora of details about other candidates, you will hear something like, "Well, you all have similar educations and experience, but there are some differences in computer skills. As you know, the ability to troubleshoot our system is a secondary but still very important part of the job description." Hmmm, it might have been described as secondary in an ad, but clearly it's more important than you thought. Time to sell your computer skills, big time.

Are there any specific areas in which you believe my qualifications are lacking?

Do you have any reservations about my ability to do this job?

You're asking the interviewer for very specific feedback: lack of the pertinent degree, not quite enough experience, experience with a firm smaller than she would like, etc. Her answer should enable you to "spin" your credentials so they mesh better with her requirements. Other versions of this same question might take slightly different tacts:

Do you have any concerns I haven't adequately eliminated?

Given my qualifications, skills, and experience, do you have any concerns about my ability to become an important member of your team?

Is there anything in my background, education, skills, or qualifications that concerns you?

Is there anything else I can tell you that would help you make the decision to hire me?

This is another variation that I use because it craftily, but directly, implies your interest in the position, puts you in the position of "helping" rather than selling, and attempts to "close" the sale . . . all at the same time.

There is, of course, a not-so-fine line between appearing confident and being an arrogant boor. Adjust the level of aggressiveness to the tone of the interview. If you've done a good job establishing rapport with the interviewer and are having a comfortable, conversational interview, there's no reason to come off like a fire-breathing dragon when it's time to close the sale:

> **I think we've had an excellent talk and I'm very interested in this position. Where do we go from here?**
>
> or
>
> **When can I expect to hear from you? If you are unable to call me before then, would it be all right if I call you before the end of _____?**

If the interviewer said he'd call Wednesday and doesn't, that's not a reason to lose sleep. Everything might be all right; a phone call the next morning might offer a credible excuse: "Oh, Ron, I'm so sorry I couldn't get to you yesterday, as promised, but I had to put out some raging fires." So arrange ahead of time to call him if you don't hear. You'll sleep better.

> **How am I doing? Do you think you will be recommending me to move on in the process?**

Hey, it worked for Ed Koch, though I think it may come off a trifle too brazen (maybe even a little too glib).

Here are two questions that are the least aggressive, though still designed to make the interviewer give you the information you need:

> **What are the key criteria you're going to use to decide callbacks? How do I measure up, in your opinion?**
>
> **What are the next steps in the hiring process?**

There are few interviewers who, when asked either of these two questions, will not make it pretty clear to the candidates who aren't making the grade that the next step is to shake hands, smile, and go on to another company: "How do you measure up, Brad? Well, I'm afraid you don't."

Likewise, those viable candidates should be given a roadmap for the rest of the process—who they should meet with next, how long the process should last, how many other candidates are still in the running.

Salespeople can be more aggressive

What if you're seeking a sales position? I've counseled *every* candidate in identifying hidden objections through probing questions, ask closing questions and, most important, ask for the offer. Don't you think it's even *more* important for potential salespeople to aggressively seek answers...and the job?

You bet it is. Questions that may seem overly aggressive to an accounting major may appear positively mild to a fire-breathing salesperson. And most sales managers *expect* salespeople to be aggressive—it's supposed to be their nature. So the closing questions can be as aggressive as you can make them (within the context of the rest of the interview, of course, and with due respect for the personality of the interviewer):

> **I believe I've demonstrated the qualifications, experience, and attitude you're looking for. So, when can I start?**

> **There's clearly a fit here. I'm ready to come aboard immediately and exceed your expectations. Can we discuss the details of my package?**

> **I'm sure we'll have no trouble dealing with compensation issues. Can we start by discussing a salary slightly higher than you advertised?**

These and similar questions that you should now be able to construct on your own have two things in common: They exude confidence and assume that the job is already won. The latter, naturally enough called an "assumptive close," is virtually *de rigueur* for any salesperson. But it is certainly a possible means for more aggressive interviewees of any stripe to "go for the close."

Getting to yes

Young salespeople are taught the importance of getting prospects to say "yes." Neophytes are often given a series of scripted, closed-ended questions to ask with the sole purpose of getting a series of yes's, on the assumption that if someone says "yes" enough, they'll fall right into the yes that matters: *"Do you want to buy my product/service?"*

Without going into the plusses and minuses of such a sales technique, let me suggest that there is an adaptation that might be appropriate in some interviews or with some interviewers. Especially, it seems to me, those who haven't conducted the clearest interview of all time or who have given you the impression that they're a little lost. Perhaps you can help them towards a decision with this technique. The following are two sample "scripts" I've created. Until the end, I'm going to assume you have done a wonderful job and the only thing the interviewer can say is, of course, YES:

> *"Mr. Barnes, have we established that I have the educational background you're seeking?"*

> *"And do I have the breadth of experience you want? "*

> *"Have my answers allayed any concerns you may have had about my abilities?"*

> *"Am I someone you feel you and your team can comfortably work with?"*

Presuming a series of resounding "yes's" in response, the sales candidate would be ready to close:

> *"So should we start discussing the compensation package and make arrangements to get cracking?"*

Here's a more detailed way to get to the same place:

"Mr. Olsen, the original ad that brought us together detailed a number of qualifications. May I go over them briefly with you?" (YES)

"I think it's important that we review what we've discussed and make sure I haven't failed to discuss an important topic, wouldn't you agree?" (YES)

"The ad specified a BA degree from a four-year college, right?" (YES)

"An English major?" (YES)

"Coursework in creative writing?" (YES)

"Internship for at least two summers?" (YES)

"Two to three years on-the-job experience in consumer magazine editing?" (YES)

"Some experience with layout?" (YES)

"It also stated that the company wanted a "go getter," someone ready to move higher up in publishing and take over the reins of the entire magazine within five years. (I didn't say this was a highly realistic script!) (YES)

"Obviously, these requirements are just the tip of the iceberg. You of course want an individual that will fit in with your corporate culture, someone you and my future coworkers will be able to get along with. Do you think I have the personality and personal style to do so? (YES)"

"Have I answered all your questions to your satisfaction? (YES)"

If at any point your questions elicit a no, you would pause, clarify the misinformation, confirm that you now understood each other, then restate the question in a way that would "restart" the series of yes's. Otherwise, you would immediately proceed to a series of closing questions:

"Can I assume from your positive responses that I am a serious candidate for the job?"

"Can you tell me where you are in the process?"

"How many other candidates would you say you still believe have a shot at this job after talking to me today?" (This is a strong close, but it's very positive and I personally like it a lot)

"Whom do I need to talk to next? May I set up an appointment with her before I leave today?"

"When do you expect to make a final decision and fill the position?"

Frankly, even an aggressive sales type should avoid being *too* pushy. Pressuring an interviewer for a decision by a specific day (or, worse, immediately) may be going overboard at all but the most Type-A companies. However, if you acknowledge that you're *being* pushy, you may get away with it! For example:

"Jim, I like you, I like the people I've met, I like the company, and I am excited about this opportunity. I don't mean to come on too strong, but I have been interviewing elsewhere and I

*am expecting at least _____ other offers before
the end of the week. Is there any way I can hear
from you before Friday?"*

The nicest thing about this question is that it makes
you seem even more attractive: "Hey," you're announc-
ing, "other companies are ready to make me an offer.
What's wrong with you?

You can always work for free

Here's a great question for use in the kind of tough
economic environment you're facing right now, a time
when interviewers are deathly afraid of making a mistake and choosing the wrong finalist:

*"I realize you have a very difficult decision to
make, but because you've indicated you need
at least a week to do so, would you object if I
came in first thing tomorrow morning and actually showed you what I can do? I wouldn't
expect payment, of course, until you officially
hired me at the end of the week."*

Speaking as someone who has hired hundreds, and
who still sometimes worries that I've missed something
and may be making the wrong choice, it would be mighty
hard for me to pass up this "free trial offer." It completely
devastates the competition! It effectively puts off the decision for a week-a week during which you are in the
office, working away, making friends and influencing
people, while your competitors are, what, sitting by their
phones? You have taken control.

Do you really think the decision was being made in a week? Who cares anymore? You are in a position to force the decision to be made in a week. You have closed the pre-sale and put yourself in an unbelievable position. Is there any question in your mind as to whether you'll be hired at the end of the week? Only if you really can't do the job, they hate you, or you hate them. In which case you've saved everyone a lot of grief and only "wasted" a week!

When it just isn't working out

We've all been there—an interview that is obviously not working. Maybe it's the interviewer, maybe it's you, maybe it's the weather, maybe it's God's cruel joke. Whatever. The interview is not going well. You are sorely tempted to get up, thank the interviewer, and run, not walk, to the safety of your bedroom.

Don't leave. Excuse yourself, perhaps for a bathroom break. (Hey, I know it's not usually done, but right now we're trying to salvage an interview that's going down in flames faster than the Hindenberg). Compose yourself. Give yourself a pep talk. Then go back in there and work your butt off to sell yourself.

You may actually be completely wrong for the job, which is why the interview is not going well. But that doesn't mean there aren't *other* jobs at that company. Or other *jobs* at other *companies* the interviewer knows about.

Don't give up prematurely. Your very attempt to salvage the situation may result in a surprising reaction by the interviewer.

Questions to ask yourself after every interview

Kate Wendleton, founder and president of The Five O'Clock Clubs, a national job-networking organization, has her counselors ask a series of questions of every candidate when they return from an interview. I heartily recommend that you ask yourself the same questions (and take notes on your answers):

How did it go?

What did they say?

What did you say?

How many people did you see?

How much time did you spend with each?

What role does each of them play?

Who seemed the most important?

Who is the hiring manager?

Who is the decision maker?

Who seems to most influence the decision?

Who else did you meet (secretaries, receptionists, department heads, peers, etc.)?

How quickly do they want to make a decision?

How do you stack up to your competition?

What objections did you have to overcome? Do you think you did so successfully?

How badly do you want this job?

What's the next step according to them?

What is *your* plan?

Chapter 7

Questions TO GET the BEST DEAL

Ask a few "experts" about dealing with salary issues during an interview and you'll undoubtedly receive a range of advice. Some advise bringing the topic to a head as soon as possible. Others suggest avoiding the subject entirely, as if getting a paycheck were some unspeakable practice, inquiring about that filthy lucre somehow "indelicate."

Common sense dictates a course somewhere between these two extremes. I recommend that you avoid bringing up the subject of salary yourself during your screening and selection interviews. If the interviewer brings it up, do your best to deflect her. It's really in your best interest to avoid getting down to the brass tacks of salary negotiation *until an offer has been made*. Not talking about salary at some point is, of course, ludicrous. But talking about it at the *wrong* time is just foolish.

So don't discuss dollars and cents until after you've convinced the interviewer that you're the best person for the job. Until you've made it over all the other interview hurdles, the interviewer is still assessing your ability. And he or she is probably still seeing other contenders as well—some whose talent may come cheaper than yours.

The interview is a classic buy-sell situation. You are trying to sell yourself to a company and get the best price you can. The company is making sure that it wants to buy what you're offering, and, naturally, hopes to pay as little as you'll accept.

If you can stand apart from the crowd of applicants, if you can convince the employer that an extra couple of thousand dollars would be well-spent on a dynamo like you, then one of the only sure ways *not* to get it is by hanging a price tag around your neck too early in the proceedings.

If the interviewer is loathe to bring up salary during the early stages of an interview, then your bringing it up is a sure way to make him feel you are self-absorbed and interested solely in the money.

Would you buy something from a salesperson who only wanted to impress upon you how much something cost?

Of course not.

Why would a company hire someone only interested in seeing how much he could get?

I, and most experienced hiring managers I know, have at least one story about candidates who asked only about salary, benefits, and days off...just before they were thanked and shown the door. *None* of these subjects is one to raise when an employer asks, "So, do you have any questions?"

But even if an interviewer tries to pressure you into naming a specific number early in the game, avoid committing yourself. Instead, name a very broad range. You might say, "I believe a fair wage for this kind of position would be between $60,000 and $68,000." And the higher the salary, the broader the range.

Be sure the bottom end of that range is no less than the minimum salary you would be willing to accept for the position.

You should, of course, have a pretty good idea of what your particular market will bear long before you walk into the interview. If you don't know the high and low ends in your area (city and state) and industry, do some research. Make sure you know whether these figures represent just salary dollars or a compensation "package" that may include insurance, retirement programs, and other value-added benefits.

If you're a woman, make sure you know what men who are doing the same job are making. You're bound to find a discrepancy, but you should request and expect to earn an equivalent salary, regardless of what women predecessors may have earned.

It's important, so I'll say it again: Timing is everything. *You have nothing to gain by discussing dollars and cents before you've convinced the employer that you're the right person for the job. In other words, the best time to discuss salary is **after** you get the offer.*

What if the interviewer blinks first?

You can always tell when an interviewer is paying people too little. This kind of interviewer will bring up salary early on to determine whether she can afford you before spending the time to interview you.

Okay, that might not always be the reason that the subject of salary is broached too early. It might just be that the interviewer is inexperienced or has a premonition that you'll want more than he can afford to pay.

Whatever the reason, if the subject of salary *does* come up too early, sidestep it. Remember: It can't possibly do you any good to discuss salary before you've sold the employer. One of the following replies might prove useful:

"I have an idea of the salary range for the position from your ad (or from what the recruiter said). It sounds like a reasonable range to me."

"I'm willing to consider any reasonable salary offer."

"I'd feel more comfortable discussing salary after I understand my responsibilities better. Is that alright with you?"

"From what I know about the position and the company, I don't think we'll have any trouble agreeing on a fair salary."

"I'm well aware of what salaries are for this position within the industry. I'm sure that if salaries here are comparable, we'll have no trouble coming to an agreement."

Fielding the offer

So, you're an ace candidate. You have impressed the interviewer so much that a couple of days later you get an offer by phone.

You're delirious. You want to shout with joy. You got the job!

Don't get too carried away just yet. You've captured the high ground in your search for a job. Now you want to take advantage of that.

Even if you've been out of a job for months, this is *not* the time or place to let your desperation show, so avoid gushing, "Gee, this job sounds so gosh-darned wonderful I can't believe you're going to pay me anything! Just give me an office and a phone and I'll work for the sheer fun of it!"

I stressed earlier that the interview is a buy-sell situation. Now that the company is sold on you, *you're* the one who must make the decision to buy.

Get the complete offer in writing with all details spelled out. But be careful—I actually once interviewed someone who was so mistrustful she insisted that I confirm, in writing, that she be allowed to wear sneakers to the office every day...and that I had to notify her 24 hours in advance if I expected her to dress up for any reason. Otherwise, she intended to wear jeans in the winter and a T-shirt and shorts in the summer. And *that* had to be confirmed too.

Can you say, "I'm sorry, I just changed my mind about hiring you?" I did.

Take your time. You should never—I repeat, *never*—accept a job the minute it's offered to you. Even though you've probably thought about little else since your last interview with the employer, and have thoroughly made up your mind that you will accept the job if it *is* offered, politely inform the interviewer that you "need some time to consider it."

You could say you want to sleep on it, or think about it over the weekend, or talk it over with your spouse or "adviser."

Most companies will push you for a fairly quick response—they have probably interviewed other promising candidates for the position and don't want to lose *them* if you turn them down.

However, don't act before *you're* ready to. Tell the person making the offer that you need a short time to think it over, thank her for thinking so highly of you and agree on a day and a time that you'll call back with your answer.

Questions to ask when you've gotten an offer

I'd like a little time to think about your generous offer. When would you like me to get back to you?

When would you like me to start (earliest or latest)?

If I have further questions, whom should I contact?

You indicated that my base pay would be _____ plus a bonus would be payable quarterly based on specific criteria you've outlined. I understand the medical benefits. You've also told me that I shouldn't expect consideration for a company car for one year. Are there any other items we should discuss to make this offer complete?

Especially if the money isn't all that you'd hoped, you are looking for hints about how flexible the interviewer (or the company) can be about perks: Is a better title negotiable? Will they pay for your cell phone? Give you an advance against travel expenses? Reimburse your graduate school tuition? Buy you a laptop computer to use at work, at home, and on the road?

As I'll discuss a little later in this chapter, it is imperative that you consider the whole compensation package, not just the salary, when evaluating an offer.

What to do if you don't like their offer

You know the salary range for the job on offer. You either discovered it through your research, found out by asking a recruiter or Human Resources, or asked the hiring manager directly.

If you are offered a salary close to the top of that range, consider it a compliment and don't think too hard about pushing for more money. You don't have that much to gain anyway—particularly in today's performance-based job market.

But if you're offered a salary at the floor of the range, you may certainly consider making a case for a better deal. You may say something such as, "I understood that the position was paying as much as $84,000, and yet you're offering me only $77,500. You told me that you've interviewed several candidates for the position. Well, you've selected me because of my management and financial expertise, as well as my experience working with plastics. Therefore, I believe a salary of at least $81,000 is reasonable for me to expect." (By *not* pushing for the very top of the range in this example, you have made it very easy for the interviewer to see it as a "win-win" situation and give you what amounts to an immediate $3,500 raise.)

Never couple asking for more money with an explanation of why you "need" it. Rather, always couch such a request within a declaration of the "extra value" the employer should expect in return. Remind him of the cost savings and other benefits he'll enjoy when you come on board. For example, you might say: "I was able to cut my previous employer's expenses 10 percent by negotiating better deals with vendors. I think it's reasonable to expect that any additional salary we agree on will be more than offset by the savings I will bring the company during my first few months on the job."

If the interviewer won't budge, and seems to have at least reasonably valid arguments as to why, ask when you will receive your first salary review. If the answer is on your anniversary date, see if you can push for an earlier review to make up some of the shortfall between the offer and your expectations: *"I am very flattered by the offer, though I wish we could have agreed on a slightly higher salary. Could you give me my first salary review in, say, six months, rather than 12?"*

This is a rather easy concession for the interviewer to make. He will think that he is getting you for only half the difference between what you want to earn and what he wants to pay.

Look for win-win solutions. If the employer is adamant about not increasing your salary, he may be amenable to a company car or some other perk that works for you and for him.

Unless you become overheated and frantic, employers expect negotiation. You will not lose the offer just because you try to negotiate—it may actually be the final test!

Even if you're disappointed, but have decided to take the job, make sure everything ends on a friendly note. Otherwise, you're leaving a bad first impression and you may be under the microscope or on a short leash right from the start.

If you become too intransigent, you may even force them to change their minds! After all, you're already showing them you're not a team player by arguing over every single detail and not giving an inch on anything, no matter how inconsequential.

They're offering a package, not just a salary

If you are already an experienced worker at any level, you are aware that salary is only one part of the compensation package you can expect. But even if you are an entry-level candidate, I encourage you to analyze the entire value of the compensation package before making any decision. Some companies provide very generous benefits packages—including stock options, dental care, company cars, free lunches, and more—even to the rank and file. If these benefits don't fatten your take-home pay, at least you won't have to pay for them out of your own pocket.

Most company vacation policies are fairly standard—two weeks for the first three years, three weeks thereafter. Some companies offer "comp" time in exchange for a great deal of overtime. Some match employee deposits to retirement plans. Some require employees to contribute something toward health insurance. A number of benefits—such as profit sharing—may only be available to senior-level employees.

You should have learned something about the company's standard benefits package early in the game. If, at this stage, you find the offer abysmal, why are you still considering that company?

If there are any other questions you feel will affect your decision about whether to accept this job, you had better ask them now, while you are still considering the offer!

Here's a comprehensive list of all forms of compensation, which, obviously, are far more extensive than just salary and a holiday bonus:

Basic compensation

Base salary
Deferred compensation (401(k), SEP-IRA, etc.)
Incentive compensation
    Performance bonus
    Sales commission

> Sales incentive plans
> Shares of stock

Stock options
Matching investment programs
Profit sharing
Signing bonus
Timing of first review

Perquisites

Company car or gas allowance
Continuing professional education
Conventions—paid attendance and expenses
Employee discounts
Executive dining room privileges
Executive office
Expense account
Extra and/or other types of paid insurance
Extra vacation days or weeks
Financial planning assistance
First-class hotels or air travel
Furlough trips for overseas assignments
Memberships
> Country club
> Luncheon club
> Athletic club
> Professional associations

Paid travel for spouse
Personal use of frequent-flyer awards

Private secretary

Tax assistance

Tuition assistance

Relocation expenses

Closing costs, bridge loan

Company purchase of your home

Discounted loans/mortgages

Home-buying trips

Lodging while between homes

Mortgage funds/short-term loans

Assumption of mortgage prepayment penalty

Mortgage rate differential/housing allowance

Moving expenses

Outplacement assistance for spouse

Real estate brokerage fees

Temporary dual housing

Trips home during dual housing

Related to severance

Consulting fees after termination

Insurance benefits after termination

Severance pay and outplacement, including extra weeks/months of severance

Questions to ask yourself before saying "Yes!"

Let's review some of the basic questions you asked yourself very early on (didn't you?): What's the purpose of your job hunt? To get an interview? Only if you enjoy collecting unemployment on the way to your next performance. To get a job? Well, sure, but what *kind* of job? How about getting a job that you will actually like, that you can actually do, that ties in with your values and interests, that offers future opportunities, etc.? Yes, Grasshopper, you are beginning to see the light.

Don't get me wrong. There are certainly situations in which you can't be choosy and, indeed, getting a job, *any* job, is preferable to cruising local trash bins. But those situations should be dire circumstances—if you don't get a job tomorrow, your family doesn't eat. Don't "create" those circumstances in your head and convince yourself that a job offer, any job offer, is something to leap at. What good (again, except under the direst of circumstances) is getting a lousy job that you will wind up hating in a month...or less? Do you really want to restart this whole job hunt from scratch? I didn't think so.

So as tempting as it is to accept an offer without a lot of deep analysis, especially if the money is exceptional (or, at least, more than you thought you were going to get), take the time to go through that analytical process and ask the right questions:

Do I really want this job?

Does this job mesh with my long-term career plans, or is it an abrupt detour? Does the described "career path" mesh with my own?

Can I really do this job as described? Will I enjoy doing it as described?

Does the company's/department's culture match my strengths? Will I comfortably fit in with the team, department, etc.?

Do I really like/respect the person I'll be working for?

Do I like the people with whom I'll be working or whom I'll be managing?

Is there anything else I need to know about *anything*—the company, department, job description, boss, team, subordinates, colleagues—to assure myself that this is the right move?

And what's the purpose of asking questions? To get the job by showing how smart you are and how much research you've done? Only partly. Yep, that other part (and don't sell it short!) is to make sure the answers make you smile, not wince! A fast-paced environment where merit is quickly rewarded? Great! Just what you want,

Ms. Type A. A cutthroat department where you'll need to spend half your time covering your butt and the other half sucking up? Don't think so.

No matter how good the offer and how happy you are, don't think only of the present:

> **In this job or department, on what basis are raises and bonuses awarded?**

> **Could you tell me more about how bonuses are structured? How much is based on my individual performance? How much on the performance of the department, company, division, etc.?**

The job description is negotiable?

Remember that you are not just negotiating your compensation, you are also negotiating what particular work you will do for that salary (plus benefits and perks, of course). There is plenty more room to "define" a job the way *you* want to than most employers will ever admit. The more they want you, the more flexible they may prove to be.

Why don't you want me?

Invariably (that is, at least once in your lifetime!) you will not be offered a job, no matter how many times you've gone back, how many interviews you've had.

There are many possible reasons. The job was more fluid than you thought—the company is rethinking its strategy and isn't even sure they're hiring anybody. Or they're redefining the job (which may or may not work in your favor). Or the executive who has to sign off on the decision went to the Bahamas...for three weeks. Or the hiring manager simply can't decide between you and another candidate. Or two. Or three.

There are two kinds of rejection that occur during the job-search process: the kind you expect and the kind you don't. The first is easy to understand and describe. I once interviewed for a vice-presidency at a prestigious international travel magazine. I knew things had not gotten off to a good start when I met the interviewer at a restaurant—he looked like he had just stepped out of the pages of *Gentlemen's Quarterly*. And I...well, I didn't. I wasn't wearing jeans and I didn't have nose hairs creeping out of both nostrils, but I was clearly in a different sartorial league. I saw the evaluating look in his eyes and knew I had already taken my first strike. (As it turns out, it was probably three strikes right then and there. The person he hired was a lightweight salesperson and manager but a charming rake with a monstrous closet of designer duds.)

Within 15 minutes, I knew I had definitely struck out. In answer to a very specific question, I happily noted that I did indeed have the unusual experience he said he needed. Had done it for six months at a single job. There was then a long pause, as he unsuccessfully scanned my resume for any hint of that job...and I realized I would be leaving long before dessert.

The latter reason for rejection was my utter stupidity (not to mention my duplicitous attempt to "sanitize" my resume to avoid a charge of job-hopping). It clearly taught me a couple of lessons and was, therefore, an experience that helped me later land a more appropriate job.

And my lack of sartorial splendor, which clearly cost me the job before I had read the menu? It was an unstated but highly implied requirement for the job that I failed to even contemplate. I just didn't think of clothes as anything more than something you wore because society didn't condone running naked around the office. Not only would I never get a job where model-level "grooming" was a keenly desired trait, I would never *want* such a job.

The lesson learned was more subtle but far more important: Think about the real requirements for the job and make sure they match not just your desires but "you." If I had thought for even a moment in earnest, it should have been apparent that the audience for such a magazine would be decidedly upscale, as would the advertisers, as should the image of the salesperson trying to *sell* those advertisers. I work hard, work fast, and do great work. But I am not going to give anyone the impression that I am Ralph Lauren incarnate. Nor, if I want to have a happy life, should I try.

What if you believed in your soul that you knocked the interviewer's socks off? If it comes as a genuine shock that you didn't receive an offer at the top end of the salary range, let alone no offer at all? Go through your memory and your interview notes to see if you missed something. Did the interviewer hint that he had a problem with something that you simply ignored in your haste to talk about something else?

But be aware that there are many reasons this might have occurred, and certainly not all of them are even remotely connected to your interview. The job description may have changed without your knowledge. Another candidate with much stronger credentials may have waltzed in and delegated you to that sad "Strong Number Two" position. The position may not even have been available—the interviewer may have concocted a quick one- or two-day "experiment" to see if there was someone out there better than the employee he already had. (In my experience, this happens in smaller companies all the time, especially family-run firms.) You may not only have had to impress him more than the other candidates, you may have had to beat out the guy already on the job!

Will you ever know for sure? Probably not. Not that long ago, I would have given you a bunch of advice on how to get the interviewer to give you some hints "so I can do better the next time." Unfortunately, the hiring landscape has changed pretty dramatically in the last couple of decades. Employers are so scared of being sued that it's difficult for another employer to get more than "name, rank, and serial number" (name, title, and salary) when calling for a new employee reference. Believe me—I'm the only person in my company who is allowed to talk to someone asking for a reference. And I say virtually nothing. Absolutely nothing even remotely negative. Which is, after all, why they've called me in the first place—to ensure they aren't hiring someone I just fired for embezzlement, sheer craziness, or killing my cats. Sorry, no other info. Good luck. Better you than me. Let the cats out...quick.

If you're working with a recruiter or headhunter, he or she may be in a position to get more information than you would ever on your own, but, again, don't count on it.

What if you left the interview with the distinct impression that there were unexpressed objections. You tried. You asked probing questions. You all but begged for feedback. Nada.

Then follow up is even more important. If you know what the objection is, answer it in your follow-up letter. Then write another, somehow bringing up the objection again and giving yet another reason why it isn't valid. And then another.

The danger, of course, is that you're tilting at windmills of your own creation, that there *is* no real objection, just some of the above possibilities (vacation, indecision, etc.). In which case, all you're doing is drawing the interviewer's attention to some glaring hole in your resume or education or qualifications...none of which he noticed before. But thanks to your help, you are now a non-candidate!

How do you follow up? Following an enthusiastic recounting of how much you want the job, how perfect your qualifications seem to mesh with their needs, etc., etc. (either in a letter or during a telephone conversation), here are two smart questions to ask if a job offer doesn't materialize:

Is there more information I can give you?

I've been giving a lot of thought to (something you discussed) and have developed some (ideas, sketches, plans, proposals). May I come in and discuss them with you?

Your negotiating "cheat sheet"

☐ **Wait until you receive an offer** before you discuss salary, benefits, vacation days, etc. Deflect any question of salary that comes up early in the interview with an answer like this:

> *"From what I know about the position and the company, I don't think we'll have any trouble agreeing on a fair salary."*

Or

> *"I'd like to know a little bit more about the job responsibilities and the level of expertise you're expecting before I feel comfortable discussing a salary."*

☐ **Research compensation levels.** Look within your industry and locally—within your city and state. If you don't already know the salary range for the specific position you're considering, find out. You need to go into salary negotiations armed with this information.

☐ **Know your worth.** Once you receive a solid offer, you know that the company wants you. They have decided you are the best candidate they have met. This puts you in a position of power. If they balk at your initial salary demand, remind them of the specific benefits they stand to gain from hiring you.

❐ **Get it in writing.** Especially if you negotiate a complex, nonstandard salary/benefits package. Be sure you have something in writing—either a letter or memo from the employer, or one you've sent that's been accepted—before you give notice to your current employer.

❐ **Negotiate the perks.** Make sure you understand the value of *all* the potential benefits in the salary/benefits package. Benefits can vary widely and, depending on your level, could be a substantial part of your package.

❐ **Go for the top.** If that is more than the company will pay, the interviewer will counter with another offer. Work toward a compromise from there. Employers expect some give-and-take. You will not make them angry if you remain calm and professional.

Once you've accepted an offer

How do you convince someone who's just offered you a job that she absolutely made the right decision? Ask one of these smart questions:

Are there any upcoming events occurring before my start date in which I could participate?

The more social, the better. You really want to get to know everyone after they've let their hair down. (And if they never let their hair down, there's a message there too!) So a company picnic is great. A departmental, Friday night, let's-have-a-beer-together is nice, though socially tough if you're not a butterfly. It would be most beneficial if you could attend one of these before you make a decision, but that's unlikely. However, if there's a big press conference or similar corporate event, you could always ask to attend. A little exposure to the "big wigs" to see what they're really saying in public as opposed to what they told you in the interview may prove enlightening.

What could I do before I start to jump start my entry into the department?

Is there any reading I can do to prepare for my first day (reports, memos, whatever)?

Both of these (and similar) questions will confirm to the interviewer that he has made the right decision. Look at that passion! That interest! That aggression!

The Five MOST IMPORTANT QUESTIONS

In the Introduction, I boiled down 101 tough interview questions to four. Well, I'm going to boil down the many smart questions I've suggested you ask to six. When all is said and done, here's what you absolutely want to know before you accept any job:

Can I do the job?

Are you really qualified? Be honest with yourself, because if the answer is no, sooner or later it will not be a secret to your boss!

Do I *want* to do the job?

They may love and want you, but you'd better be sure this is a job you can be passionate about. If not, but you plan to take it anyway, you should at least be honest and *know* you are compromising for a reason that is valid to you...like, you have to eat.

Does this job fit in with my long-range plans?

The more solid and thought-out your long-range goals, the easier it is to create a directed and targeted career *path* rather than simply a series of jobs that fail to build upon one another. Just as you can and should direct the interview, you must control your own career path. Make sure you have honestly analyzed whether this job fits in with your own goals.

Will I fit in?

Did you like your boss? Did you like the people you'll be working with? Those you'll be managing? A job is not simply a set of functions, it's a collection of environments created by all the other people that work at the company. You may be totally qualified for and challenged by the job itself, but if you can't stand any of the people, how long do you think you're going to last?

Can I live on what they want to pay me?

I've lectured you enough about keeping money in perspective, but one does have to live. If your ideal job won't even pay the rent or the mortgage, you have a problem. But the biggest problem is if you haven't bothered to think about your financial needs at all.

Do I feel secure taking a job at _____?

Doubling your salary may be wonderful. Stock options could make you rich. Or you could find yourself back on the street in a month if you haven't bothered to ask yourself this question. Always evaluate the compensation package in concert with your analysis of the health of the company. It doesn't matter how much they promise to pay you if they're heading towards bankruptcy.

Appendix

Smart QUESTIONS TO ASK

About the company

Are you currently planning any acquisitions? (111)

Do you have a lot of employees working flextime or telecommuting? (129)

How fast is the company growing? (126)

How many employees work for the organization? (111)

Please explain the company's organizational chart. (125)

What are the key challenges facing the company? (132)

What are your goals in the next few years? (112)

What are your key markets? Are they growing? (111)

What are your leading products or services? (110)

What are your plans and prospects for growth and expansion? (112)

What do *you* like best about this company? Why? (112, 134)

What growth rate are you currently anticipating? Will this be accomplished internally or through acquisitions? (111)

What has been your layoff history in the last five years? Do you anticipate any cutbacks in the near future and, if you do, how will they impact my department or position? (111)

What have you enjoyed most about working here? (134)

What have you liked least about working here? (134)

What is your hiring philosophy? (112)

What is your ranking within the industry? Does this represent a change from where it was a year or a few years ago? (112, 126)

What is your share of each of your markets? (111)

What kinds of people seem to succeed in this company? (134)

What major problems or challenges have you recently faced? How were they addressed? What results do you expect? (111)

What products or services are you planning to introduce in the near future? (110)

What sets you apart from your competitors? (126)

Which other companies serving your markets pose a serious threat? (111)

Will you be entering any new markets in the next couple of years? Which ones and via what types of distribution channels? (111)

About the department

Could you explain the organizational structure of the department and its primary functions and responsibilities? (112)

How many people work exclusively in this department? (112)

To whom does my boss report? (112)

To whom will I be reporting? (112)

What are its current goals and objectives? (112)

What are its specific objectives for the next three months? (125)

What has the turnover been in the last couple of years? (129)

What kinds of people seem to succeed in this department? (134)

What problems is this department facing? (112, 132)

What would you most like to see changed in this department? (127)

With which other departments would I work most closely? (112)

About the job

Are there after-hours business events I will be expected to attend? (129)

Could you describe a typical day in this position? (113)

Does this job usually lead to other positions in the company? Which ones? (114)

How advanced/current is the hardware and software I will be expected to use? (114)

How did this job become available? Was the previous person promoted? What is their new title? Was the previous person fired? Why? (113)

How do you see me working with each of the department heads? (127)

How do you see my role evolving in the first two years? (132)

How has this job been performed in the past? (132)

How long has this position been available? (113)

How many hours a week do you expect your star employees to put in? (130)

How many people will be reporting to me? (113)

How much budgetary responsibility would I have? (130)

How much day-to-day autonomy will I have? (114)

How much travel should I expect to do in a typical month? (129)

How will we work together to establish deadlines and objectives in the first months of this job? (136)

How would my performance be measured? (127)

Is relocation an option, a possibility or a requirement? (113)

Is there no one from within the organization who is qualified for this position? (113)

Please tell me a little bit about the people with whom I'll be working most closely. (114, 130)

Please tell me more about your training programs. Do you offer reimbursement for job-related education? Time off? (113)

What decisions can I make without oversight? (131)

What do you think my biggest challenge will be? (132)

What is the first problem I should tackle? (136)

What is the one thing I can do right at this job do assure my success? (137)

What kind of training should I expect and for how long? (113)

What skills are in short supply here? (136)

What specific goals should I set for my first three months on the job? (136)

What three things need immediate attention? (136)

What will my days be like? (125)

What would be the most logical areas for me to evolve into? (132)

Where will I be working? May I see it? (113)

Would I be able to speak with the person who held this job previously? (113)

About the process (including "closing" questions)

Are there any specific areas in which you believe my qualifications are lacking? (143)

Before you're able to reach a hiring decision, how many more interviews should I expect to go through and with whom? (114)

Can I assume I am a serious candidate for the job? (150)

Can we discuss the details of my package? (146)

Can you tell me where you are in the process? (150)

Do I remind you of another employee who succeeded at this job? (136)

Do you have any concerns I haven't adequately eliminated? (144)

Do you have any reservations about my ability to do this job? (143)

How am I doing? (145)

How do I compare with the others that have interviewed for this position? (142)

How many other candidates have you interviewed? How many more will you be interviewing before you expect to make a decision? (114)

How many other people would you say are serious candidates for this position? 142)

How much time have you set aside for interviews before you make a final decision? (141)

How will you weight your subordinates' input? (128)

Is there anything else I can tell you that would help you make the decision to hire me? (144)

Is there anything that is stopping you from offering me this job right now? (142)

Over what period of time will additional interviews take place? (141)

What are the key criteria you're going to use to decide callbacks? (145)

What are the next steps in the hiring process? (145)

What kind of feedback does your boss expect you to give him? (128)

When can I expect to hear from you? (145)

When can I start? (146)

When did you start interviewing for this position? (138)

When do you expect to make a final decision and fill the position? (150)

When may I meet some of my potential colleagues (or subordinates)? (127)

Where do we go from here? (144)

Whom do I need to talk to next? (150)

With whom will I be meeting next (names and job titles)? (114)

About upcoming interviewers

How long have they been with the company? (115)

What are their ages and family situations? (115)

What are they like? (114)

What is their history with the company? (135)

What issues are important to each of them? (114)

About your boss's "style"

How do you define success? (134)

How do you measure your own success? (134)

How would you describe your management style? (133)

In your experience, are there particular types of people you seem to work better with than others? (133)

What do you think your responsibility is to develop your people? (134)

What kinds of people seem to succeed working for you? (134)

What particular traits do you value most in your subordinates? (133)

What's your philosophy about "mistakes"? (134)

When's the last time you got really angry at one of your subordinates? What was the cause? What did you do? Has anything similar happened since? Did you react differently? (133)

After every interview

How badly do you want this job? (154)

How did it go? (153)

How do you stack up to your competition? (154)

How many people did you see? (153)

How much time did you spend with each? (153)

How quickly do they want to make a decision? (154)

What did they say? (153)

What did you say? (153)

What is *your* plan? (154)

What objections did you have to overcome? Do you think you did so successfully? (154)

What role does each of them play? (153)

What's the next step according to them? (154)

Who else did you meet (secretaries, receptionists, department heads, peers, etc.)? (154)

Who is the decision maker? (154)

Who is the hiring manager? (154)

Who seemed the most important? (154)

Who seems to most influence the decision? (154)

After receiving an offer

Are there any upcoming events occurring before my start date in which I could participate? (175)

If I have further questions, whom should I contact? (160)

Is there any reading I can do to prepare for my first day (reports, memos, whatever)? (176)

What could I do before I start to jump start my entry into the department? (176)

When would you like me to get back to you? (160)

When would you like me to start? (160)

Agencies and recruiters

Could I meet with others you've placed at this company? (94)

Do you see any problem with the company meeting my financial needs? (93)

How integral to the company's success is my department? (94)

How long has this job been open? (93)

How long have you been working with this company? (91)

How long will the interview process for this job take? (93)

How many people have you placed at this company? (92)

How many people would be reporting to me? (92)

Is a written, detailed job description available? (92)

Is the interviewer my potential boss? (94)

Is the interviewer the decision-maker? (94)

Is this a new position? (92)

To whom would I be reporting? (92)

What can you tell me about the culture of the company? (94)

What else do I need to know? (95)

What happened to the person who previously held this job? (92)

Before you accept an offer

Can I really do this job as described? Will I *enjoy* doing it as described? (167)

Do I like the people with whom I'll be working or whom I'll be managing? (168)

Do I really like/respect the person I'll be working for? (168)

Do I really want this job? (167)

Does the company's/department's culture match my strengths? Will I comfortably fit in with the team, department, etc.? (168)

Does this job mesh with my long-term career plans, or is it an abrupt detour? Does the described "career path" mesh with my own? (167)

During an informational interview

Can you direct me to others at your company whom you think I should meet? (90)

Do you know anyone at the organizations I've targeted? (89)

How can I learn more about this field? (89)

How can I meet others in this field? (89)

How did you get started at this company? (88)

How do you spend your day? (88)

What are your duties and responsibilities? (88)

What do you like least about your job? (88)

What do you like most about your job? (88)

What is the best way to get started in this field (or at this company)? (89)

What kind of person do you think is right for this kind of work? (89)

What skills are in short supply here? (89)

Where would you see me fitting in at a company such as yours? (89)

Human Resources

Are there any challenges facing this department right now? (100)

Can you tell me more about what I'd be doing on a daily basis? (99)

Can you tell me something about my boss? (99)

Can you tell me something about the interviewer? (99)

Can you tell me something about the people I'll be managing? (99)

Can you tell me something about the people with whom I'll be working? (99)

Do you have a written description of the position? (100)

Do you have any concerns about my abilities? (98)

Does the company have a mission statement or written philosophy? (100)

How quickly are you hoping to fill this position? (99)

How would you describe the corporate culture? (99)

How would you say I stack up against the other candidates you've interviewed? (99)

Is this a new position? (100)

What are your recruiting plans this year? (97)

What happened to the last person who held this job? (100)

What other positions at the company should this job prepare me for? (101)

What particular attributes or skills do you want a candidate to possess? (98)

What's a key thing about the company you'd like me to know? (98)

Where are you in the decision-making process? (99)

Yourself

Are you a good loser or a bad winner? (39)

Are you a risk taker or risk averse? (38)

Are you overqualified? (101)

Can I do this job? (177)

Can I live on what this company wants to pay me? (178)

Can you achieve your ultimate career path in your current company? (64)

Can you comfortably afford your current lifestyle? (60)

Describe your personality. (38)

Do I feel secure taking a job at ____? (178)

Do I want to do this job? (177)

Do you have the qualities generally associated with the level of responsibility you're seeking? (44)

Do you mind traveling frequently? (49)

Do you rise to a challenge or back away? (39)

Do you tolerate differences? (39)

Does this job fit in with my long range plans? (178)

How can you make yourself more marketable in today's competitive job market? (40)

How can you transfer skills and experience you already have to a completely different career? (65)

How do your positive attributes match up with the qualities you believe necessary for success? (44)

How does your current job differ from your ideal job? (65)

How does your self-description match that of the culture of the company you're considering? (56)

How many of your positive qualities do you want to use in your job? (45)

How well do you interact with authority figures? (50)

How would you describe your dream job? (65)

How would your friends describe you? (39)

If you had to spend 40 hours a weeks doing a single activity, what would it be? (39)

In what size city do you want to work? (48)

In what size company do you want to work? (49)

Is a formal employee-training program important to you? (49)

Is a tuition reimbursement plan important to you? (49)

What additional education or training do you need to achieve your dream job? (65)

What are your goals and aspirations? (40)

What are your key values? (38)

What are your long-term goals? (37)

What are your passions? (40)

What are your short-term goals (37)

What are your strengths (37)

What benefits do you require? (49)

What can you learn from past bosses? (50)

What do you least like doing? (38)

What do you most like doing? (38)

What games and sports do you enjoy? (39)

What has caused you to break up friendships? (39)

What have you already done to accomplish your short-term goals? (37)

What in your personal life causes you the most stress? (39)

What in your personal life gives you the most pleasure? (39)

What is important to you? (37)

What is your current standard of living, and are you happy with it? (60)

What kinds of friends do you tend to have? (39)

What kinds of people do you dislike working with? (40)

What kinds of people do you enjoy spending time with? (38)

What kinds of people do you like working with? (40)

What kinds of products/services/accounts do you want to work with? (49)

What salary would you like? (49)

What specific things do you require in the job you're seeking? (37)

What standard of living do you aspire to? (60)

What were your favorite subjects in school? (39)

What would it take to transform yourself into someone who's passionate about every workday? (40)

What's the lowest salary you'll accept? (49)

Where (geographically) do you want to work? (48)

Who are you? (37)

Will I fit in at this company? (178)

Is there anything else you need to know about *anything*-the company, department, job description, boss, team, subordinates, colleagues-to assure yourself that this is the right move? Ask those smart questions now!!!

INDEX